PSYCHIC COP

PSYCHIC COP

KEITH CHARLES
with
DEREK SHUFF

BLAKE

Published by Blake Publishing Ltd,
3 Bramber Court, 2 Bramber Road,
London W14 9PB, England

First published in Great Britain in 1995

ISBN 1 85782 120 3

Printed in Fin.

1 3 5 7 9 10 8 6 4 2

Contents

DISCLAIMER
The views expressed in this book
are those of the authors, and not
of the Metropolitan police

I dedicate this book to the
loving memory of Mathew who
went home to Heaven
on 16 November 1994

FOREWORD
by Jenny Seagrove

You only have to look at the night sky, brimful with stars, and wonder what's beyond 'the beyond' or contemplate infinity to know that there must be some other 'angle' on life and why we're here. I suspect we don't know the half of it.

So when I read Keith's story, written simply and directly, with an honesty that leaps off the page, and he declares, 'this is no cranky mishap', it just reaffirmed everything that I already felt and believed.

That Keith is a policeman as well as a psychic is very reassuring. When you meet investigating officers, and I have met a few, they bring with them calm common sense, straightforwardness and the emotional detachment that are absolutely necessary in their job.

The common perception of a psychic tends to be of a rather vague, perhaps slightly unstable, crank, whose eyes will suddenly glaze over and who starts talking or writing a lot of mumbo-jumbo. Yet how untrue this is. Every psychic I've ever met has been direct, 'together' and rather more uncomplicated than the rest of us. Only occasionally do you come across a charlatan, in it only for money and showbusiness.

If Keith was a weirdo, prone to flights of emotional fancy, I know the police force would have let him go years ago. Instead, they even see fit to use his gift when the occasion arises. This is a remarkable man, with a remarkable talent and a remarkable story to tell.

I have had a few psychic experiences myself. Not with Keith, though, as I've only had the pleasure of sharing a rather dressy police dinner with him (and a few hundred others), which was not exactly conducive to psychic communications!

The occasion that moved me most happened on television in front of about four million viewers! It was breakfast television and, sitting on the sofa opposite me, was well-known psychic Doris Collins.

My paternal grandmother had died three days before and I was wearing her wedding band on my finger.

All was proceeding smoothly. I had plugged the film I had been asked to talk about, and Ms Collins was in full flow. Suddenly, she broke her sentence, turned to me and said, 'I have a message for our young friend here.' (I must add, this was a few years ago!) Then she proceeded to reassure me that my grandmother was all right and to tell me things that only the inner circle of my family could have known. After the programme, she continued with more messages from my granny. From that moment on I have never doubted that there is a whole other 'world' out there. I just wish I could get my phone line as clear as Keith's!

As well as being entertaining, Keith's book is reassuring. Death is no longer a dark abyss but a new horizon with something exciting beyond it that we can all look forward to journeying towards when this life ends; a kind of spiritual progress to 'the next stage' whatever that may be.

I'm looking forward to my next meeting with Keith and, through him, to having a chat with my mum who crossed that new horizon when she died nearly a year ago. Who needs British Telecom?

Jenny Seagrove
London

INTRODUCTION

There is nothing spooky about being able to talk to those in the spirit world, any more than there is anything spooky about an aunt in Adelaide, Australia talking to someone in Britain over a telephone link from the other side of this world. Both are miracles of communication.

It's just that many people find it more acceptable to believe the voice on the end of the telephone line is an aunt because she says so and because the telephone is now an understandable and therefore acceptable means of communicating with someone. We have everyday proof that the telephone works, even though most of us don't understand how.

On the other hand, with contact to the spirit world through a clairvoyant like me, the 'miracle of communication' is not so clearly defined so it is not so readily accepted. However, that doesn't mean it is any less genuine!

Let us first of all understand what is meant by 'clairvoyance'. One dictionary defines it as: 'The supposed power to see or know things that are out of the natural range of human perception. Acute intuitive insight or perceptiveness'. The word comes from a French word meaning 'clear-seeing'.

Three other words need defining, too – 'spiritualist', 'medium' and 'psychic' – because these words are about as spooky as the word 'telephone' and achieve much the same purpose. Understand their true meaning and you take away much of the mystery of contacting an aunt who didn't just go to live on the other side of this world, but to the spirit world. Whether she is now in Australia or the spirit world, it may not be possible, or convenient, for her to make contact with the loved ones she has left behind, but if she can, and wishes to do so, you can be sure she probably will.

I am clairvoyant and a spiritualist. I am a human telephone link with those who have passed into spirit.

Let's take 'spiritualist' first. The dictionary meaning of this is: 'The belief that the dead communicate with the living, usually through a medium'; 'medium' – 'A person thought to have powers of communicating with the spirits of the dead'; lastly, 'psychic' – 'A person who is especially responsive to extra-sensory and non-physical mental processes or forces'.

You can prove that the voice on the other end of a telephone line is your favourite Aunty Flo because if you have any doubts, you ask her personal questions to which you already know the answers. But how do you know that the spirit messages coming to me, your clairvoyant, are really from a now-deceased Aunty Flo? It is done in precisely the same way. I ask her questions and she establishes her identity and credibility with the often very personal information she sends back.

The spirit world is seldom interested in telling us on Earth how to run our lives but they do want to be reassured that their departure from the physical life has not caused their loved ones lasting grief. They have found happiness and they want those they have left behind to be happy too. That is why so much of the information passed on by clairvoyants like myself may seem to be trivia, other than to those to whom it is directed.

I recall one public meeting on a British tour, when a man in the audience quickly recognised a former navy pal I had linked with. There was a lot of banter for a few minutes, until I suddenly became aware (I often get mental pictures of my spirit links) of Arthur, in spirit, kicking his feet out in front of him. 'Why is he kicking out his feet, as though he's showing them off?' I asked the man in the audience.

After he'd stopped laughing so heartily that the rest of the audience were looking back over their shoulders to see what all the hilarity was about, the man called back to me: 'That's because Arthur lost both his feet in a shipping accident when he was alive. Now he's over there he has obviously got them back again!'

I thought the audience would never stop clapping their approval. Even I had to chuckle, but it goes to show that we still retain a sense of humour in the spirit world.

My point is that evidence is the all-important factor when it comes to being a good clairvoyant, as I believe myself to be and as others have told me they believe me to be. Casting modesty aside for a moment, I attribute what success I have as a spiritualist to the fact that I am a trained and practising policeman, a true psychic cop, if you like, which is what I am often nicknamed by my friends and even by a number of my police colleagues. As a detective, I know the importance and necessity of obtaining hard evidence. I'd have been fired from the police force many years ago if I'd dealt only in hearsay or plain gossip instead of hard facts.

The same goes for spiritualism. Too many clairvoyants deal in useless information that could apply to anybody.

In my opinion the late Doris Stokes was one such person. Sometimes I'd sit and listen to her and wonder how she became so famous but I've since put that down more to her personality than to her ability to give meaningful information to her clients. 'Your husband Fred sends his love. Oh, and he says you can throw his socks away now. He won't need them any more!' Doris would say. Well, of course the audience loved it because she made them laugh, and people like to think they can relax and laugh at a psychic meeting but I used to wonder how many of them, on their way home, would realise how very little real information Doris's spiritual contacts had passed on. When I am in spirit contact, I probe and probe, as I would in my work as a murder squad detective.

This introduction is to help you, the reader, to understand what you will read in the following pages. If you have never been to a 'psychic evening', that will not matter. Spirits will not materialise in your sitting room, so you can happily take this book to bed for night-time reading!

So much rubbish has been written about life after death – whether there really is; why there is not. Self-proclaimed spiritualists are themselves much to blame for the larger part of the mush that gets into print and is put out over the airwaves and on to the theatre stages throughout the world. It is no wonder that so many people dismiss it as mumbo-jumbo.

So let's clear the air a bit. I want to take to task those who I believe have used spiritualism for the wrong reasons, usually that they see it as a quick way to make money. I intend to name some of Britain's best-known psychics as overrated fortune tellers, with about as little intuition and psychic perception. I intend to take the Spiritualist Church to task for keeping itself firmly rooted in the nineteenth century.

With the twenty-first century just around the corner, with more open-mindedness and a breath of fresh air flowing through the world of science, we shall soon be seeing some startling new evidence of the sustainability of the human soul. Evidence that, on death, it does not expire like the dying flame of a candle but that its energy, as with all matter, cannot be destroyed. The spirit crosses the dimensions of time and life itself to continue its spiritual 'cleansing' beyond our current earthly comprehension.

If, in time, there is to be a more worldwide acceptance of life after death, as I believe there will be, then the mystique must be swept aside. The rogues who give spiritualism a bad name must be exposed. More modern and rational thinking must be allowed expression. Spiritualism needs a spring-clean and I hope this book is seen to be a start.

Keith Charles

Tragically, on 16 November 1994, as this book was being prepared for publication, Keith Charles's eldest son Mathew was killed in a road accident.

In Chapter Eleven, Keith and his other two sons pay their tender tribute to Mathew, a very gifted clairvoyant in his own right.

CHAPTER ONE

GARDEN WALKS WITH THE QUEEN MOTHER

For me, life as a policeman has never been dull. I have helped to protect the Queen at Buckingham Palace, Prime Minister Edward Heath when he was at No 10, the Queen Mother at Clarence House and Prince Charles and Princess Diana when they married at Westminster Abbey, as well as many diplomats in their embassies.

These were largely protection posts around London, where, in some cases, I stood on duty with a loaded handgun inside my tunic, the weapon discreetly hidden from public view. Sometimes it was definitely quite scary, although not for reasons you might imagine.

Although Buckingham Palace has its own regular police officers, when one went sick or was away on holiday, I would get called in to do duty in the palace grounds. One night, although I knew it was irregular, I was sitting in a little lodge in the grounds, which we used for our breaks. It had a small, one-bar electric fire and was about the closest we could get to a bit of comfort on a cold winter's night. In between patrols I stopped off in the lodge to read snatches of a horror book I had with me.

Brrrr – it was chilly and very windy. The leaves on the trees and bushes were rustling and shafts of bright moonlight flickered through the trees from behind the fast-moving clouds. I couldn't help thinking how creepy it was, made worse by reading my horror story.

Then I really did become quite nervous, as though I sensed that something wasn't quite right. Was it my psychic perception at work? Had I picked up the vibes of an intruder in the grounds of Buckingham Palace? Although I knew it was a very rare occurrence for someone to break in, it had happened before.

I heard rustling coming from some nearby bushes. This was for real; it was not the wind playing tricks. As the disturbance in the bushes came closer, I felt

the hair on the back of my neck prickle in antici-
pation. I was only a young police constable at the
time and I decided I had to go and take a look and
confront the intruder if that's what it was. Gripping
the handle of my truncheon tightly, I moved towards
the bushes. There was a scuffle and suddenly the
bushes parted and this 'thing' jumped out at me – it
was a big, black labrador on patrol with its police
handler!

Phew! I must have looked like death warmed up
but I was very relieved to find it was a friend. I told
the handler that he'd scared the hell out of me. As for
the dog, its handler told me it was just being friendly.
It knew I wasn't an intruder!

Being a young copper, just up from Brighton, it
gave me quite a kick to do duty at the palace. This
was the Queen's home, probably the best-known
home in the world, and here I was, coming from a
fairly humble middle-class grocer's family, on duty
protecting Britain's most important lady. At first it
was all a bit unreal.

The Buckingham Palace garden parties were quite
something for me. I loved them even though I was
working. All those lords and their ladies; the rich in
their flash cars, posing in fine clothes, and, yet, what
amused me was that, no matter who they were, they
all had to queue up with their tickets to get in. It was
a great leveller. I couldn't help thinking they were
really no different from a crowd of football support-

ers waiting for the big match, although there was rather less chance of hooliganism breaking out when the gates opened.

One palace garden-party day was warm and sunny, with a strong breeze blowing, and as I stood on duty at the front entrance to the palace, I could see the ladies in their light summer dresses having some difficulty keeping their fancy hats on their heads. One lady lost the battle as a gust snatched her hat from her head and sent it skimming across the palace forecourt like an airborne flying saucer. It landed at my feet and I instinctively stamped my foot down on its rim to stop it from being blown on. However, there was no way I could pick it up immediately because I was trying to hold back a crowd of sight-seers. Before I could do anything about the hat, a royal car came by – and ran right over it!

The whole thing was a millinery disaster. The white-ribboned, broad-brimmed hat was now flat-tened and dirtied beyond repair. I shall always remember the look on that woman's face as she lifted this tatty bit of cloth from the tarmac, taking the opportunity to give me a long, hard look of contempt. The accident was simply unfortunate and I felt sorry for her. She was understandably very angry, very embarrassed and also disgusted with me that I hadn't been much help.

When I was stationed at Cannon Row police station, one of my favourite duties was on Horse

Guards Parade, at the back of 10 Downing Street which, as everyone knows, is the prime minister's home. I just loved the rehearsals for the Trooping of the Colour ceremony and the sound of the pipes and drums. At 6 a.m., with the mist swirling in off St James's Park and the pipes sounding across the open guards ground, it was really spiritual. It sent tingles down my spine. I'd just stand there lapping it up; it was so mystical.

The Queen Mother has always been my favourite royal so when I first met her it was all the more special for me. I was doing duty at Westminster Abbey, as one of a number of police cadets forming a guard of honour.

The Queen Mum came out and when she was in front of us we all stamped to attention and saluted but then she stopped and began speaking to some clergymen. We had expected her to walk right past and down the path to her car. We didn't know what to do, whether to hold our salute or drop it! The cadet next to me whispered, 'What shall we do?'

I said, 'Hold it', which we did.

Then the Queen Mum moved on and, as she passed, she turned to me and said, 'Thank you for waiting, officer.' I felt ten feet tall.

I was to meet the Queen Mother again, this time actually inside the grounds of Clarence House, her official residence. We had a little police post in the grounds of Clarence House and on this particular occasion I was on duty inside the hut, enjoying a cup of tea. Suddenly the door opened and, bold as brass, in walked the Queen Mother!

I'd have been embarrassed if my own mother had suddenly walked in and caught me having a cup of tea when I was on duty, so you can imagine how I felt with the Queen Mother standing in front of me, smiling kindly. I jumped up, saluted and snapped out, 'All correct, Ma'am.'

She just melted me with her smile and her loveliness; it was like being hypnotised with charm! She looked at me and said, 'I wondered if you might like to accompany me on a walk round the garden?'

Well, who could refuse such a request? So off we went. We just wandered slowly round the gardens looking at the flowers. It was wonderful. I didn't chat much but I spoke when she spoke to me. Out of politeness, I walked just slightly behind the Queen Mother, although I got the impression that she would have preferred me to walk more alongside her to make it easier for her to comment on the flowers.

After about fifteen minutes I was back at my post, hardly able to believe what had just happened.

Colleagues later told me that the Queen Mother often popped in to see her police officers at Clarence House, to say 'hello' and, occasionally, would even join them for a cup of tea.

I pick up auras and I was very aware of the warm red aura which surrounded the Queen Mother. This showed strength, loyalty and considerable stubbornness – not the kind of lady to argue with because I could sense that she could be very firm. However, I have to say she made me feel very comfortable in her presence.

In our police training we had never been told how to behave in the presence of royalty so on my garden walk with the Queen Mother I was just myself. With royalty in general, I have always worked on the principle of not speaking unless spoken to and being very polite.

You will often see a policeman standing outside 10 Downing Street. Well, I can tell you that I have done that, too, and it can get very boring! I was there when Downing Street was open to the public and it was very much a favourite sight for tourists.

I wonder how many of them met the mass murderer Dennis Nilsen? He killed fifteen men and is now serving life imprisonment in the top-security wing at Whitmoor Prison, Cambridgeshire. As a former policeman he once did the same job as me outside No 10, and at the same time. Makes you think, doesn't it!

One little old lady came to see us every day. She'd walk up, say 'hello' and give us sweets. She called us 'my boys'. A real diamond, that one.

One winter's day another policeman who was on duty at No 10 with me decided we needed something to stimulate our circulation. As it was snowing quite heavily, he chucked a snowball at me. It clipped my nose. There was nobody about in Downing Street so I hurled one back, which splattered over his chest. In no time at all, snowballs were flying in all directions. Unfortunately, one of mine wasn't very well aimed and I must have accidentally scooped up a stone inside it because when it hit one of the prime minister's windows, it cracked the glass. The window didn't smash but a big crack appeared down one side.

Luckily, it hadn't been heard inside No 10 because the PM didn't poke his head out of an upper window and not even a servant came to the door to find out what was going on. We decided in this instance that discretion was the better part of valour and we kept the mishap to ourselves. I suppose a workman doing routine maintenance found it in due course and replaced the broken pane.

We also had fun in Downing Street with the tourists. They would come up and say, 'Gee, is this where the prime minister lives?'

When I said yes, they'd sometimes ask, 'Is it real?'

If I felt a bit bored and a tiny bit mischievous, I might go on to say, 'No, in fact what they have done here is build a false frontage,' pointing out that that was why there were only three house numbers: 10, 11 and 12.

I would add, 'I expect when you saw Downing Street on your televisions in America you thought this was a big street? Well, as you can see, it is only a replica.' I would kid them on that there was nothing behind the false frontage other than scaffolding, and explain that the prime minister really lived in the country.

They'd take it all in. All the coppers there played this game because it was a great way to pass the time on duty! Sometimes we'd take it to extremes just to see how much rubbish tourists would believe. When asked if I was armed, I'd say, 'We are trained to kill at thirty yards – with our truncheons!'

I especially liked taking the mickey out of Americans. Americans who want to know their way to somewhere tend not to ask directions by saying, 'Can you tell me the way to wherever?' They just say, 'Piccadilly?'

I was on duty one night in Whitehall, with a fellow copper named Steve, when an American came up to him and said, 'Piccadilly?'

Steve replied, 'Leicester Square.' The American repeated, 'Piccadilly?'

Steve answered, 'Oxford Street.' And so it went on.

Frustrated by Steve's responses, the Yank then said, 'Hey, Mac, just tell me how to get to Piccadilly.'

'How did you know my name was Mac?' asked Steve.

'Gee, I guessed,' said the Yank.

'Well, guess your way to Piccadilly,' snapped Steve. It was hilarious. I just burst out laughing.

I don't want to give the impression that, as policemen, we were contemptuous of tourists. That was not true at all. I loved all the different people and their cultures. We would just string them along a bit and make our lies bigger and bigger until they realised we were kidding them on. It was a laugh and they really enjoyed speaking to British policemen.

The fact that we might be armed intrigued many people. I joined the police force in 1969 and when I walked into the canteen at Cannon Row police station I would see many policemen walking around wearing handguns. It was quite frightening at first. On duty at No 10 I was armed myself.

I had to go on a gun training course and learn to shoot standing up and lying down. I had a Walther PPK and was given a magazine primed with seven bullets, which I kept in a holster under my jacket. I never used my gun, although I did have to take it out on several occasions when hunting for armed suspects. Things are a lot different now and there is much more extensive training.

I had wanted to be a policeman from the age of fifteen. I left school in 1966 and joined the police cadets in May 1968. In the intervening two years I had three jobs. I worked for my aunt and uncle in their Brighton fruit shop, as an order clerk in a local printers and I had another job as a roofing estimator. However, my heart was set on being a copper, so when I was accepted to the police cadet training school at Hendon for six months, I couldn't have been happier.

The happiness was a bit short-lived, though, because at Hendon they really put me through it, with a lot of discipline, twenty-mile runs, night treks, the lot. It was tough, like being an army cadet. Even so, I still enjoyed the life.

After Hendon, I was sent as a qualified police cadet to Sunbury-on-Thames to get some experience in a police station. After that I moved on to Southall police station.

As a cadet, I didn't have a warrant card, just a piece of blue paper authorising me to do school crossing patrols. It was embarrassing standing there with a lollipop sign in my hand. All the roughnecks had a field day, wolf-whistling and generally taking the mickey out of me. Being a lollipop police cadet was a bit of a bash to my ego. It was a bit like being a mounted policeman with only a donkey to ride.

It was around this time that my cadet friend, Kevin Kerman, broke his neck. One moment he was a hero after he rescued a drowning girl from the Thames, the next he fell off a roof beam during training, with tragic consequences.

Kevin was a basketball player, a good sportsman and athlete and a great-looking boy, and suddenly he was paralysed from the neck down. He went straight to Stoke Mandeville Hospital where I visited him regularly, although I have to say that I've lost touch with him now. Even so, I would like him to know that I still think of him.

I believe I am a compassionate policeman, which is what I always try to be. I was a CID officer at Paddington police station the day a young man was arrested for stealing a car. He was about twenty-five and asthmatic. Members of my own family suffered from asthma so I knew it needed to be taken seriously. An enthusiastic young police constable, with only about twelve months' service, had taken this young offender out of his cell to try to give him some air while he waited for the ambulance.

I was dealing with another prisoner but I took the young asthmatic a cup of tea. I could see he was in a bad way, breathing heavily and with great difficulty. I knew he needed urgent help so I told him I'd boil some water in the kettle and he could sit over it and take in the steam to give him some relief.

'You can't do that. He's my responsibility,' said the young PC. I told him I would accept responsibility and moved the lad over to the steaming kettle, where I also rubbed his back while he breathed in the hot vapour. Then he went off to hospital in the ambulance and I forgot all about the incident.

Some time later, the lad came back from hospital in handcuffs and I heard him say to his escorting officer, ''Scuse me, before you put me into a cell, I'd like to speak to that officer over there,' pointing towards me. He came over and said he just wanted to shake my hand for what I did for him. I really appreciated that little gesture.

I did my stint in uniform but I knew I really wanted to be in the CID. I enjoyed working with criminals. That was much more interesting than the prospect of spending the rest of my life reporting missing tax discs, defective tyres and traffic offences. Nor did I want to spend the rest of my life standing at the front door of No 10.

When all the workers are in bed, London is a different place, even quite a pleasant place. I enjoyed my night duties. It was also a time when the unexpected often happened.

Imagine, if you will, two uniformed coppers, in step, hands behind their backs (you know, the way they walk in *The Bill* and all the best films), and that was PC Keith Wright (Charles is my clairvoyant name) and PC Paul Garforth casually making their way along Whitehall at 05:30, returning to Cannon Row nick for breakfast.

We were quite alone – no traffic, no people, not a movement anywhere, other than this one pigeon crossing the road on foot, just ahead of us! 'That stupid pigeon is going to get run over,' I told Paul.

In his broad Yorkshire accent, he answered: 'Don't be bloody silly, pigeons don't get run over. They fly off!'

No sooner were the words out of his mouth when a taxi came from a side turning into Whitehall – slap into the pigeon. However, it wasn't killed. It just lay there in the road, flapping its wings. Now, I hate birds, and this one fluttering away in the road very close to death disturbed me. I told Paul one of us would have to kill it and it wasn't going to be me. He said it wasn't going to be him either.

Another copper, named John, was on duty by Admiralty Arch, so I asked him down to take a look at this poor pigeon. Would he put it out of its misery? 'Not me, mate,' said John.

So there we were, three uniformed coppers bending over a half-dead pigeon in the road in Whitehall, arguing over which one of us was going to have the courage to finish it off! In the end, Paul agreed he'd do it. He told me to hold the bird and he would crack it with his truncheon. I insisted that John hold the pigeon but he wouldn't, so I had to. I held the poor thing at arm's length while Paul took aim. I turned my head as he struck with the truncheon – and missed.

'For heaven's sake, ring its neck,' I told Paul but he wouldn't. By this time I was feeling quite ill and I dropped the poor bird on the ground. Paul lashed out again, missed the pigeon and struck the pavement such a heavy blow that it split his truncheon in half. Now Paul would have to explain to his station sergeant how he broke his truncheon trying to finish off a pigeon in Whitehall!

A couple of days later, the station sergeant asked

me if I'd seen the report by this new officer to our station, in which he had produced a lovely story about how he broke his truncheon? I told him it was true and that I had been there when it happened. Even the sergeant had a chuckle but he said he couldn't possibly file the report as it would get him the sack!

We never lived down that incident; it was the talk of Cannon Row police station for months. As for the injured pigeon, it was all too much for it. By the time we'd organised ourselves it had died without our help.

Ironically, only once have I been contacted by the spirit of a dead police officer. He was an incredibly tall bloke, even for a policeman. He just stood there, looking at me and, in a gruff voice, gave me his first name which was Arthur. When I asked for more details, he turned and showed me the number on his uniform. Sure enough, someone in the audience knew him. He was hardly one of my more co-operative spirits but then I suppose he thought I should have been out pounding the beat, rather than chatting to him over the psychic airwaves.

In case you are interested, few criminals who have passed into spirit seem interested in making my acquaintance from beyond. One, however, just a little cocky that he was now well beyond the reach of the law, came through and gave me his name as Albert. He said that in his lifetime he had been a bit of a magpie and had spent quite a lot of time in what he

15

described as 'one of Her Majesty's holiday camps'.

In 1971, after nearly two years in uniform at Cannon Row, I was accepted as a detective and posted to Kingston. It was there, in Wimbledon, that I met many tennis stars, as well as comedians Bobby Davro and Gary Wilmot. Perhaps, in some strange way, this was the beginning of becoming what many people and newspapers now call me: 'Psychic to the Stars'.

CHAPTER TWO

THE WORLD'S ONLY SERVING PSYCHIC COP

I am a policeman who also became a psychic, which gave the British police force something to think about! They hadn't come across a psychic copper before and they were not quite sure what to make of this strange new interest of mine when I came to register it as the police rules and regulations required me to do.

The police are regularly swamped with offers of assistance from self-proclaimed psychics. Well-meaning callers they may be, but few of them are genuine clairvoyants. We deal with these people politely, our attitude being that when, for example, a murder is under investigation, any offer of help is gratefully received and considered, whatever its source.

So now, by day, I am Detective Constable Keith Wright investigating and questioning the living. (Wright is my real name. My clairvoyant name is derived from Keith William Charles Wright.) Away from my police work, mostly at night, I am a medium who questions the dead. No wonder it confused my bosses!

When I reported my active interest in spiritualism, my immediate guv'nor, a chief superintendent, called me to his office for a chat. 'Tell me what this is all about,' he said. I had no idea at the time how my superiors would react, probably with horror and considerable alarm was my first thought but I could not have been more wrong.

First, I had to explain to my guv'nor what was meant by spiritualism. After all, I was certainly the first Metropolitan policeman to ask to register as a psychic and they didn't know how to categorise me. I had to register my new interest as a business because I would be receiving payment from a source other than the police.

In the end it was agreed that I should register as a medium which was especially satisfying because it meant that the police officially recognised my psychic work.

My colleagues were intrigued too. They wanted to know why I was involved. What was I getting out of it? Did I really talk to the dead? Many of them were quite cynical because they hadn't ever met a psychic before, let alone been to a psychic meeting, and here I was, one of their police colleagues!

I didn't need to be too clever a detective to realise that stopping off at the local spiritualist church and talking to those in the spirit world was not most coppers' idea of a great evening out! I knew that my guv'nors found the fact that I did just that hard to understand too. To be fair, though, in the end they were happy for me to go on with it as long as it was in my own time and not when I was working. I have never abused that agreement. On the other hand, I have never been told not to use my psychic gift in my work as a Metropolitan police detective, which I have done a number of times.

I believe that being a psychic makes me a better policeman and that being a policeman makes me a better psychic. To have the two together must make me unique because I know I am the only registered serving psychic policeman in Britain – and probably in the rest of the world. There was one in New York but he retired some years ago.

I am a better psychic by being a policeman because my police training has taught me how to question everything I am told. As a police detective, I deal in hard facts, not hearsay. I know how to seek out these hard facts through diligent questioning and I am not fobbed off with evasive rubbish. When a spirit comes through to me at one of my meetings, it gets asked all the right questions until it gives me detailed answers.

I believe I am a better policeman by being psychic because I can bring another dimension into my work – the dimension of clairvoyance, a gift I have developed and used to considerable effect in both my psychic and my police work. I have to say at this point, however, that spirit messages do not make good police evidence. My boss would not take too kindly to me going to him and reporting that a certain spirit I'd contacted the night before had imparted important information. No witness, no statement, no use!

On the other hand, my psychic 'eye' often leads me in certain directions. My reputation for this is known in police stations in the London area and, because of my psychic demonstration tours around Britain and the publicity I seem to attract, to regional crime squads, too. On numerous occasions police colleagues have asked me if I have any 'thoughts' about their own cases and sometimes I have been able to help. Like the time a detective friend came to see me with a ring that had belonged to a murder victim. When I held this ring, I kept getting a particular name which later turned out to be the name of the murder suspect. However, my 'evidence' on its own was quite useless.

It would have been more helpful if I had been able

to say, 'Spirit is telling me that the man stabbed his victim with a knife and that that knife is in the toilet system of the house next door!' Bingo! The detectives recover the knife, find the fingerprints and arrest the murderer. In evidence, they would then just say that, as a result of information received, they went to a certain house and found the murder weapon. This is the only way psychic information can be used in police detection.

One interesting piece of psychic information I learned related to the mysterious disappearance of estate agent Suzy Lamplugh.

Maureen, my ex-wife, used to put things into envelopes then, when I came home, I would hold the envelope and say what I believed was inside. On one occasion she gave me an envelope and I kept getting the name of a road in Fulham. I was also aware of a playing field nearby. Then I saw a girl I knew to be Suzy dead in the basement of a big house in Fulham. I knew she had been killed there. We checked out the road in the London A to Z road guide and there was a playing field nearby, just as I had seen it clairvoyantly.

I was so unnerved by the clarity of this vision and the accuracy of the information which came to me that I contacted the detective inspector in charge of the Suzy Lamplugh case and passed on what I had 'seen'. I never heard any more about it. Deep down he may have thought I was a nutter and so did nothing about it but I can only say what I believe.

Then there was the case of Lee Boxall, a boy who went missing in Croydon on his way to a football match. The detectives working on that case had over fifty people, calling themselves mediums, ring up with their theories. One of the officers at the station told me that his guv'nor wanted to see me to get some idea if any of these mediums were credible and known to me.

One or two had come up with some quite interesting stuff but the police were worried that one of those ringing in might be a suspect sounding out the police to find out what they knew — or didn't know. I was able to help by identifying some of the mediums.

To give you some idea of the kind of useless information the police can be told, one well-known medium rang to say that the boy's body would be found within fifty miles of water. That was it, nothing more. You cannot go anywhere in Britain without being much more than fifty miles from water! That kind of call just wastes police time. My prayers go out to the Boxalls and all families in similar situations.

Some mediums, knowing that I am a policeman as well as a medium, ring me with their spirit messages or their dreams. Most of them mean well and they pass on their information feeling that they might prevent someone from being arrested if they don't. I always ask them in future to question the information they intend to give to the police before actually doing so. Does it answer the kind of questions a policeman would ask them? If it does, fine, ring in. If not, then save their phone bill.

When I am interviewing a suspect, or people connected with a crime, I can get very strong feelings as if spirit is around me, watching over me, guiding my questioning. When it makes me go goosepimply, I know I am on to something or someone.

Once, when I was working on a rape which happened at Kingston Hospital, one of the lads on the crime squad was asked by Cannon Row police to go and arrest a man for common assault. I told the arresting officer that we were looking for a rapist and I made it my business to find out what kind of common assault was involved because I was getting very strong vibes that this same man was the one I wanted for the hospital rape. I learned he had tried to drag a girl into his car. I went to his home but he wasn't in. His mother was there, however. She was a nice lady, really charming, and invited me inside. I just knew I was in the right house and that the same young man was responsible for the two offences. Spirit confirmed my feelings.

One of my ways of questioning sometimes is to give people the impression I have met them before, even though I know I haven't. This is a technique for asking questions without raising suspicion. How else am I going to get the information I may need? If my casual form of questioning confirms I am barking up the wrong tree, then no harm has been done to anyone. On the other hand . . .

I was chatting away to this lad's mum and I said to her, 'I know your boy, don't I?' I told her I thought I used to play football with him. 'He has a really hairy chest,' I said. 'He used to work at so-and-so.'

The lady was stunned. 'Well, yes, he does. How did you know that?'

I knew then that spirit had put me on the right track and into the right house. The man was subsequently arrested and charged.

It is difficult for me to describe the difference between intuition and spirit help because they are both 'feelings' that enter my mind. Yet I know there is a distinct difference.

Was it psychic or was it intuition when the name Ricky came into my head during a murder inquiry I was involved in at Wimbledon?

The victim had been a taxi driver. At the station, there was a book in which we had to enter the name of any suspect we thought might be involved. I didn't know this Ricky, whose name just came into my head, but I did know his brother.

It turned out that Ricky didn't actually do the taxi driver murder but when we investigated him we discovered that, on the same day, he had kidnapped a girl, taken her into Richmond and killed her. A few days later he told another girl what he had done, then killed her too. Ricky was arrested, brought back to our station and charged, but he hanged himself in Brixton while on remand.

There was no doubt that my psychic instinct triggered me into action when a friend and I were on our way to work at Cannon Row police station. As we walked past Big Ben, a kid on a scooter drew up just ahead of us. For some reason, I said to my mate: 'Come on, he's nicked that!' We went over to this bloke and I asked him where he'd got the scooter. He threw the machine at Mickey and raced off down the road, through the traffic lights towards the Houses of Parliament, with me hot on his heels. I caught up with him against the waist-high wall that runs alongside the Houses of Parliament, beside the Thames, and forced his hands behind his back. In the struggle we both nearly fell over the wall into the water! He had stolen the scooter a few hundred yards away, outside the former Greater London Council building.

In police work you develop a sixth sense but it has a lot to do with the way you are trained to look around you. I may be driving past a row of houses and I see somebody in jeans, trainers and jogging top, but standing still, looking about them. That draws my attention and encourages me to take a second look. That is not intuition, though, that is experience as a policeman.

I'd look at his shoes; look to see if he has a mate; look to see if there is a car parked nearby. So what is he up to? As I say, this is crime detection experience.

Most people would walk right past someone like that and wouldn't give him a second thought or look.

When my spiritual intuition makes me aware, it is quite different. I will hear a voice in my head say, 'Look round the corner.' I'll see a man pacing up and down. I get little leads about things I cannot even see. Or I will be driving along a road and the same voice in my head will suddenly tell me to turn left. I turn left and see somebody stealing a car. Strange little things like this often happen to me.

Humour plays its part too. I am not sure whether it was psychic feeling or straightforward human intuition that told me the reason for an elderly Hastings woman's joy when I delivered what I thought would be the shattering news that her husband had just died!

I drove over to the council estate on my own, found where the couple lived and parked my police car. At the house I was visiting, I saw a woman cleaning her windows. 'Hello, love,' she called out as I walked towards her.

'Mrs Smith?' I asked.

'Yes, love. Me old man, is it?'

'Well, yes. Could you come down?' I asked gently.

'Dead is he?'

'Well, yes,' I told her.

'OK, love, thanks,' she said and carried on cleaning her windows. I turned round and walked away. I couldn't believe it.

Three weeks later, a letter arrived at Hastings police

station from the window-cleaning lady, thanking the officer for the kind and considerate way he delivered the sad news of her husband's death. Call it what you will but my instinct told me that she came into a few bob from her old man!

I was pounding my beat late one wet night during my spell in Hastings when a couple of police mates stopped by. Ian and Ginge, a woman police officer, invited me to pop into the car for a smoke. As we sat there, quite suddenly a voice in my head said, 'A stolen car is going to come by.'

I told Ian and Ginge, 'You are going to laugh, but I can tell you that a stolen car is going to come through the traffic lights just behind us at any moment.'

In actual fact, we sat on the Hastings seafront for another fifteen minutes and not a single car passed by. Then, suddenly, a Morris 1100 appeared and drove straight through an amber light. There were four people inside. 'Come on, Ian. That's the one,' I shouted. We chased it for eight miles. Over our radio we were told it had been stolen in Sutton the previous night. I had predicted the stolen car a good fifteen minutes before it came along. Ian and Ginge couldn't believe it.

We stopped the car and arrested the occupants but I didn't have the heart to tell them I knew they were coming our way. They'd never have believed me.

From this you can see that my clairvoyance plays a very important role in my police work but, from the very start, I decided to keep my two 'hats' well apart. That is why I call myself Keith Charles as a psychic, so that my real name, Keith Wright, is kept for my police work and my personal life.

Just occasionally, however, the two come dangerously close, because there is always the possibility that at one of my psychic meetings I will meet someone I have investigated, or even arrested, as a police detective.

Once, I accompanied two colleagues with a warrant to search a house. We ended up involved in a fight with the whole family and their neighbours. It became so rough that we had to call for assistance. My friend got hit with a shovel and a girl grabbed hold of my testicles and wouldn't let go! The whole situation became quite violent and then help arrived in the shape of a police constable on a bike, peddling his heart out at a good 1.7 mph. The three of us plus PC Plod were still no match for the dozen or more family and friends lashing out at us. Anyway, calm was finally restored and the offenders later dealt with in court.

Eighteen months on, I was on a platform in a spiritualist church, giving spirit messages, when I spotted the same mum, daughter, son and one of the neighbours sitting together in the back row. I hoped they wouldn't recognise me. Afterwards they came up for a chat and the mum asked me what I did for a living. I told her I worked for the government, which wasn't really telling a lie. The daughter said my face looked familiar but she didn't twig that I was the police officer she had so uncomfortably compromised at her house when I tried to search it.

That was a real rough and tumble and I have to admit that I wasn't too disturbed when these particular people got their come-uppance in court. Just occasionally, however, I do find that my need to act strictly to the letter of the law as a policeman can conflict with my instinctive need as a compassionate medium to go out of my way to help people. Finding the right balance is sometimes difficult.

On the one hand, I have to see myself as a detective whose job it is to go out and fight crime, and on the other hand I am a man who goes to church to help people with their problems. The people I might be looking to arrest one moment, I could be helping spiritually the next. Sometimes it is a dilemma. I may not even know that they have been in trouble with the police. After all, criminals don't go around with 'criminal' stamped across their foreheads.

When my ex-wife Maureen asked me if a friend of a friend could come to see me for a reading, I agreed but I had no idea what it was about or what was going to happen. It turned out to be a very emotional experience for all of us, me, Maureen, the woman and her husband.

The woman came to our home in Molesey, Surrey. We sat in the kids' playroom where there happened to be a washing machine and a comfortable sofa. As we chatted over a cup of tea, I became very aware of the presence of a young spirit girl in the room with us. Through communication, I quickly realised that we were in Brighton. This was to do with a man named Russell Bishop, who had been cleared of murdering this girl and another in the so-called 'Babes in the Wood' murders.

I could actually see the child. She was sitting on the washing machine, dangling her feet over the side and swinging a pink elephant which the woman, her mum, told me was her favourite toy. The girl wanted her mum to know that she was happy and that her spirit was always around her mother. Personal messages were passed and it was, of course, very traumatic for the parents.

Some detail also came to light to do with the case. From my recollection, this concerned the position of the two girls' bodies when they were found and the photographs taken at the time. In any case, Bishop, who was the main suspect but who was cleared of the 'Babes in the Wood' murders at Moulsecoomb, in Brighton, was later arrested in another case, the attempted murder of a young girl. He was found guilty and was imprisoned.

I was once brought in on a murder case and had to go and tell a woman that her husband had been shot dead. He was named Eddie Roberts. He was a Londoner, and he had been shot outside a pub in Norbury. As a policewoman and I pulled up outside Mrs Roberts's house, I called upon spirit to help make this easier for me. Then I spotted a car in the driveway with the registration letters KWC – my own initials – which, to me, was a good omen.

I knocked on the door and told the woman the bad news. Then her son and daughter came home. (The daughter, Rachel, later had one of the main parts in the children's television series *Grange Hill*.)

I was made family liaison officer and came to know them very well. A couple of days after my first visit an aunt came to the house and when she saw me sitting in the lounge she said, 'What are you doing here?' I actually knew this woman as a spiritualist. First the initials KWC on the car, then this aunt turning out to be another spiritualist. It was as though my involvement was predestined. The strange course of events then continued.

I had to go to Epsom on Derby Day to make further inquiries in connection with the murder of Eddie Roberts. All I knew was that I had to go and see someone named Bill, a possible witness. As I was driving to Epsom, I kept saying to spirit, 'Come on, tell me the surname of this man. Bill who?'

I got nothing, so I continued, as I often do, to chat out loud to spirit. 'All right then, his name will be on the next lorry that comes along . . .' A lorry came into view and, as it passed, I could see on the side the words 'Taylor's Removals'.

I arrived in Epsom, at the workplace where I believed I was going to find this Bill. I ask to see Bill. 'Bill who? We've got hundreds of Bills,' said the guy I asked.

'Bill Taylor,' I told him.

'OK, he's over there.' He pointed to a man working in one corner of the building. I could hardly believe it. Spirit had really come up trumps and I muttered a quiet 'Thank you'.

I don't usually discuss this kind of help with my police pals. They are fair-minded but are a naturally sceptical lot. They sometimes have fun at my expense. The phone will ring and they will say to me, 'Keith, it's for you — but then I expect you already know that!' Or a copper will tell me that clairvoyance is a load of old rubbish, then, during a quiet moment when we are alone, will ask me if I can pick up anything on him. I get challenged to forecast who will win the 2.30 but, of course, I don't play these sort of games. I just laugh them off.

Another favourite is the play on words. When I am around they will talk out loudly about how Keith likes medium red wine or medium sweet sherry.

It gets a bit tedious at times when they come out with the same old quips but I can hardly blame them. I've never lost my cool over the mickey-taking. I have to accept that, as a medium, I am open to ribbing. Besides, I was a fat kid and learned how to handle teasing at an early age. It doesn't bother me.

CHAPTER THREE

My Psychic Awakening

Bobby Shafto was no ordinary kid. I was about eight when I first set eyes on him outside the back door of our new home in Crawley New Town. He was just standing there, a fairly short, dark-haired kid, in black shorts and creased white shirt. The most striking thing about him was his shoes. They looked a bit odd – with silver buckles on the toes. I don't really know why, I suppose it was those shoes, but the name Bobby Shafto immediately came to mind.

'Hello,' I said, shutting our back door behind me. I asked him his name.

'Norman,' he told me.

'Mine's Keith,' I said.

I suggested he join me and my friends down on the rec to play football, but he asked: 'What is football?'

That struck me as odd. I thought all kids played football, though obviously this one did not; he didn't even seem to have heard of the game. I just thought he was a new kid who had recently moved into the neighbourhood, like me, and was looking for friends.

Norman tagged along and I decided to introduce him to my mates on the field down the road where we kicked a ball around. Dave was tying his shoe-laces. 'You don't mind if my friend Norman joins us, do you Dave?'

'No, where is he?' asked Dave.

'Right here . . . Norman, this is Dave.'

Dave called out to the other two, tapping the ball to each other in front of the goalmouth. 'Hey, guys, come 'ere. Keith wants you to meet his new friend. The only problem is – you can't see him!' Dave let out a silly, snorting laugh. He apparently thought I was taking the mickey.

'Pull the other one, mate,' he said, turning his back on me.

'What do you mean, you can't see Norman? He's here, beside me.' And so he was. I could see him clearly. He was talking to me, shuffling his silver-buckled shoes around, like young kids do. What was up with Dave?

'You're going nuts!' said Dave. 'Come on, fatty, you're in goal,' he called back over his shoulder.

I thought it best to shut up about Norman. I couldn't understand how Norman was so real to me, yet could not be seen by anyone else.

Norman and I met about four or five times in all. He would suddenly appear or be waiting for me when I left my house. We'd go hopping off down the street, holding hands. It's funny how I remember so clearly holding his hand. One time when we were holding hands I took him down the length of our garden, along the outside wall, but by the time we'd got to the Jenningses' house in Cuckmead Crescent I couldn't see Norman any more, although I could still feel his hand in mine. Then, a bit further on, he reappeared again.

I can't say this bothered me. It was just that one moment Norman would be there, as physical as anything else I could see, and the next he'd become invisible, even though I could still feel his presence. I couldn't explain it but it never struck me as particularly unusual. I just seemed to accept the fact that he was able to make himself invisible to my friends, and to me, when it suited him.

So little Bobby Shafto was the first spirit I ever encountered, although at the time, I knew nothing about spirits young or old. Norman was a spirit child but I never understood who he was or why he made himself known to me. Frankly, I've never asked spirit nor have I ever really asked myself why this happened. Perhaps it was some kind of early test in my life. Or perhaps I was in the care of spirit from birth. I don't really know.

Some slightly odd things happened when I was young which have since suggested to me that, even as a kid, I had some kind of inner awareness, a sort of sixth sense which could make its presence felt in certain circumstances.

One night I had a really vivid dream. It was the sort of dream where you actually live through every detail and when you wake up you're not quite sure which is real, the dream or seeming to be awake.

Once I'd established I had been dreaming, I could recall every detail. In my dream I was playing around some shops and I found a threepenny piece and two one penny coins inside a white paper bag. A couple of days later, I was on my way to school when I heard the voice I'd sometimes hear in my head, and it said, 'Stop, and look down.'

There, on the ground in front of me, was a white paper bag and, incredibly, inside were a threepenny piece and two one penny coins. Fivepence wasn't a lot of money but to a kid of eight it was worthwhile extra pocket money.

I remember thinking that it was a bit strange to

dream of finding money and then coming across it precisely as I had dreamed I would. It was even a bit creepy so I didn't tell anyone, not even my mum. Besides, she might have taken my money!

Another time, when I was playing football, Norman told me I'd find some money in a patch of oil on the ground where an old car had been parked. I grovelled around and, sure enough, there was a sixpence. Norman was a good kid to have around.

One day a school friend and I decided to take the afternoon off and play truant. Mickey wanted us to take our bikes and ride somewhere well out of the way of the school and teachers. At first I agreed, then, for some reason, I had a change of heart. I felt uneasy about going on our bikes, so we walked.

Later we found out that, about the time we would have been in the old bicycle park, a bus had crashed there, trapping another of my pals. He lost a leg in the accident. Whether that was a psychic warning I don't honestly know, but it may well have saved me and Mickey from serious injury or even death.

Before I started seeing Norman, the spirit boy I nicknamed Bobby Shafto, I began to hear voices in my head. This is how many psychic-gifted people realise they are just a bit different from others and often, like me, they haven't liked to mention that they hear these voices for fear of being ridiculed.

My own distinctive spirit voice (it was just one to begin with) came to me during an emergency at the old Black Rock swimming pool in Brighton, which was later sold and broken up to make way for the famous marina. There were two pools: a big one for the adults and a smaller one for the kids. On this occasion I was taken there by my Aunt Violet, my mum's sister, to get me out of Mum's hair. Shirley Chapman, a cousin, came along as well with her small son Ross.

I'd say there were about a thousand people in the pool area. It was packed tight. Laughing, shouting kids ran round chasing each other. People dried themselves with large, flapping towels. Pretty girls, in skimpy swimming costumes, stretched out in the sun. I was getting my mouth round a cheese and tomato sandwich after a swim.

I think it was Violet who suddenly said, 'I haven't seen Ross for a while.' Shirley, his mum, jumped up and began looking at nearby groups, trying to spot Ross, but he wasn't to be seen. Panic quickly took hold of both adults. Nobody had to say anything, their body language told it all. They flew off in separate directions, while I carried on with my sandwich, thinking Ross would soon be found.

Then I heard a voice which seemed to come from inside my head. It was saying to me, 'He is over there.' Where? There is no way of telling precisely where when the voice is inside your head! For some reason I instinctively looked across at a boy and girl who were playing in the paddling pool – along with about eighty other small kids. 'I can't see him,' I told the voice.

It came back again. 'He is over there,' it said sternly.

I got up and found myself moving towards the young boy and girl. Sure enough, there was Ross lying on his back under the surface of the water alongside them, unnoticed by anybody. I picked him up, put him over my shoulder and carried him back to his mum.

Ross was very lucky. He coughed and spluttered a bit as his mother slapped his back to help clear his lungs. Within a few minutes he was back to normal, only playing where the adults could keep an eye on him.

The incident gave me lots to think about. I couldn't explain the voice. Was it me, talking to myself? No, I ruled that out because the voice wasn't mine. It was grown up, much more authoritative than a kid's voice. I also knew it wasn't someone standing behind me, telling me to go and look in the pool. Frankly, at the time I could not find an explanation for the voice, although I was to become ever more aware of it and the power it had over me.

Not for many years, long after I'd joined the police and when I was taking spiritual development classes, was the voice explained to me. I was told it was psychic and that the incident with Ross was my first psychic experience.

As for young Ross, ironically, he went on to become a real water baby, a Sussex county swimmer.

I am often asked to describe the voices I hear. Mostly it is difficult to do so but I will try. That first voice was rather like the voice of a strict school-teacher, in that it was not to be ignored. There was a sternness about it, a kind of discipline. For example, if you say to a child, 'Go over there,' nine times out of ten he or she will go without question. But if you say, 'Will you please go over there?' the same child might say, 'Why?'

My voice had an urgency about it. That day by the pool, by its very tone, it ordered me to go. It was a command, calm but direct, rather, as I recall, as a headmaster would talk to his pupils.

Poor little Ross! There he was, lying in about one foot of water, drowning, and nobody had even noticed. I knew what it was like nearly to drown because it was a fate I almost suffered on two occasions, the first time when I was about seven, at a Butlin's holiday camp. I couldn't swim. I'd got a bit out of my depth and was splashing furiously to try to keep my head above the water.

While this was happening, my parents and relatives were watching me from the poolside. They were arguing about who should jump in to save me! My mother said she couldn't because she had her new shoes on so, reluctantly, Dad had to do the honours.

I was fourteen when I had my next brush with

death by drowning. This time my mum and dad had taken me to Arundel in Sussex, along with a French student who was staying with us. Mum had gone for some ice cream and a small rubber ring we'd been playing with had drifted to the deep end. Not wanting to lose it, I tried to grab it but I went under. I still couldn't swim so I ended up splashing and gurgling, lashing out for the rubber ring. People were shouting out, 'That boy's drowning!' and I think they were right. Dad could see I was in difficulty but was desperately urging me to swim to the side. It was obvious that he didn't fancy making a hero of himself yet again.

In the end, just before it was too late, fully dressed, Dad jumped in and hauled me out by the scruff of my neck. My mother came back and told my father, 'Someone in the queue said a man had to jump in the pool fully dressed to rescue a drowning boy.' Seeing him still dripping wet, she chuckled, 'I might have guessed it would be you, but who was the boy? Not Keith again?'

We moved from Brighton to Crawley New Town so that Dad could take up a new job as a bread salesman with Lyon's Bakery. I went to Gossops Green primary school and so did my mum, only she went back to school to work in the canteen. She had a most distinctive laugh and I could often hear it above the singing at assembly.

It was at Crawley, as a kid, that I thought I'd never

make it to becoming an adult! It must have been around 1960 and there was serious talk on the telly and in the newspapers about the end of the world coming on a certain day. When that day came, my school mates and I thought there was going to be no tomorrow; that Crawley, Britain and the rest of the world were going to meet a rather nasty end – as had been prophesied. However, kids being kids, we decided that if we spread ourselves out close to the ground, we just might ecape the worst of it. So that's what we did.

'The end' was due during a play break and we spent much of that break flat on our stomachs waiting for the 'big bang'. Happily, it didn't happen and the rather bemused teachers filed us back in for afternoon lessons, no doubt somewhat relieved themselves that yet another doomsday prophecy had flopped.

The community centre, where my mum used to play bingo, became the Gossops Green Spiritualist Church, not that we were a particularly religious family.

My father is Dennis John Wright and my mother was Olive May Chapman before she became Mrs Wright. My younger brother John and I were born with salt air in our lungs, in Brighton, me on 22 August 1950 and John on 26 March 1954. Dad was a lorry driver working in his father's haulage business. On my mum's side, the family business was fruit and greengrocery shops. Each family employed its children so both businesses were very family-orientated.

In those early days even Brighton was a close-knit community, with everyone knowing everyone else, especially if you were a Wright or a Chapman. Both families were very much a part of the seaside resort's scene. Sometimes the fact that I was both a Wright and a Chapman was a bit of a hindrance because I couldn't do a thing without someone knowing my mum and dad and whom to inform if I stepped out of line. 'You're Dennis Wright's son, aren't you?' Or it would be, 'You're Olive Chapman's boy.'

My first memory is of my brother being born in the two-bedroomed flat which belonged to my grand-father Chapman, above one of his fruit shops in Bedford Street. Of course, I wasn't allowed to be present at the actual birth. I had to wait outside the bedroom door until John made his entrance into this world. Then the door was opened and in I went.

I was allowed on the bed but my mum told me to be careful because I had a new brother. There he was, cradled in her arms for me to inspect closely. Nurse Greenhill, the midwife, looked on proudly at the result of another of her successful deliveries! Up to the age of fifteen John was often called Johnny Pedlar, the nickname given to him by Nurse Greenhill. Later I learned that 'Pedlar' was apparently another name for 'Chapman'.

From the flat, St Mary's School, where I went, was only a short walk away, as was the Eastern public house which belonged to the father of a friend of mine named David Hawkins. When school was over, I'd often go back to the pub with David and we'd be allowed to sit on the bar top to watch children's television.

I was born at 32 West Drive, Brighton, my grandfather's house, but it was reduced to rubble many years ago to make way for three blocks of flats. I still remember the house having a three-hundred-foot-long garden. Over one hundred chickens were kept at the bottom end where there was also a greenhouse and a large pond. It was a smashing place and I have many warm memories from there.

My Aunt Violet, who had a greengrocery shop in the town, married a wrestler called Johnny Peters. Uncle Johnny and many of his wrestler friends used to come to parties laid on by my grandmother. Guys like Joe Cornelius, Jackie Pallo, Mick McManus and Georgie Kidd were always around. To a boy my age, which was under eight because we'd moved to Crawley by then, these were real heroes.

As scarce as money was, our families made sure they enjoyed themselves, using any excuse for a big party. My dad and his brothers were in a skiffle group so they soon had party times rocking along. One of Dad's musical instruments looked like a broomstick attached to a tea chest and he plucked at the wires as you would a double bass. Obviously he felt he could do better because I know that, later, he bought a proper second-hand double bass for a tenner.

The other reason my dad and his brothers were so well known around Brighton was because, apart from entertaining us at family parties, they were also a big hit in local pubs under the name 'The Wright Charlies'. Lonnie Donegan eat your heart out!

My parents were not religious so I didn't have church rammed down my throat. About the only time any of us would step inside a church was at weddings. I found our local church, All Souls, just about the most unpleasant place I had ever had to enter – cold, dark and dingy, like stepping into the sort of dank church vaults you see in a Dracula horror film.

There is no doubt that my belief in God, heaven and a spiritual life after our physical death on Earth came about during my development as a medium but I also believe that my life has been overseen by spirit since my birth, as it is with many people. Believing this and developing an affinity with spirit is something relatively few people choose to do or, perhaps, are aware they can do. My life and my work as a medium are in the hands of my spirit guides, my 'helpers' as we call them. Some call them their 'guardian angels'. Every medium has what is called a 'doorkeeper' who allows spirits in and out. As my guardian angel, mine protects me from mischievous spirits.

One of my helpers is Kurinda, a Mongolian warrior. He is very much a warrior. I don't see him very often but when I do he is always waving a big sword.

Then there is Charlie, a London barrow boy who died of tuberculosis in 1605. Tobias is a young lad who was placed in a Spanish monastery when he was only fifteen because his parents couldn't afford to keep him. He is very holy, very spiritual. I see him as a young man of about twenty-five.

Another 'helper' is Painted Horse, an Indian healing man, a big, strong character. In fact, I call him 'Runway' because when I first became a spiritualist and linked with Painted Horse, I asked him why spirits need mediums to say what they have to say?

He told me, 'We are like an aeroplane which needs a runway on which to land.' When I asked his name, he wanted to know why we on Earth always want a name. He said it wasn't important and told me to call him 'Runway' if I liked. The name stuck. Only later did he reveal his real name of Painted Horse.

Then I have a Chinese 'helper', who is like a teacher. I don't see him often but sometimes people can see him alongside me. I don't know his name. Nor do I know the name of my little blonde 'helper' but she is very pretty and very cheeky.

Mostly, in classes or at demonstrations, I tend to see Tobias, the little blonde girl and Charlie. If I see Charlie I know there is going to be a lot of good humour during the meeting. If Tobias or the China-man is there, then the evening tends to be a little sombre and emotional.

Let's take someone like Hitler. Can his spirit

attempt to communicate? The answer is 'yes', but if this spirit came through to me my doorkeeper would probably keep him out. What I am trying to explain is that evil people do not become evil spirits and get sent to an evil place to become even more evil – like a factory of evil! In Heaven, attempts will be made to put such a spirit straight. Learning will take place but there is always a chance that a spirit with a lot of evil still left in it might try to come back through a medium. However, I don't believe the spirit of Hitler would be allowed to communicate. He'd be kept away.

Whatever the risks, and of course there are some, I have never, ever regretted that I chose to take this route of spiritual development. I have so much spiritual contentment around me in this world and even more to look forward to in the next, the spirit world.

CHAPTER FOUR

PSYCHIC TO THE STARS

Elton John and Paul McCartney probably didn't know it, and may not even want to know it, but I can tell them that they are both psychic superstars! I see the aura of special spiritual energy which envelops each of them rather like a snugly fitting, misty overcoat. When he or she stands alongside Elton and Paul, developed clairvoyants will feel the glow that comes from contact with the energy of very special souls like these. They are both outstanding musicians who would make equally superb healers. Subconsciously, they will be aware of this spiritual energy.

One of the things I would like to ask both of them is have they ever noticed how people are drawn to them, not so much because they are famous but because they have what we tend to call 'magnetic personalities'? Have they noticed how children and adults have an irresistible urge to stand close to them? This happens with psychically developed people, although this ability to 'attract' others to us is seldom understood for what it often is – a strong psychic aura.

In the immortal words of Clint Eastwood as Dirty Harry, it would make my day to have a little time with both Elton and Paul to explore their undoubted spiritual gift. Incidentally, Mr Eastwood draws a blank in the psychic stakes.

It is interesting that great musicians are often imbued with psychic powers. However, are they good musicians because of their spirituality, or are they spiritual because they are good musicians? It is not a question I can truthfully answer as yet.

Two other stars of the rock and pop world whom I meet from time to time are Jet Harris, from the Shadows, the group which helped Cliff Richard to international stardom and then took itself to similar heights, and Ricky Valance, singing star of the sixties, who is still going strong. His song, 'Tell Laura I Love Her', was a chart-topper.

It is probably best that both Jet and Ricky tell their own fascinating stories and how spiritualism changed their lives for the better.

JET HARRIS

'Keith knew a friend of a friend who first invited me along to one of Keith's psychic evenings. This one was somewhere in London. I can't remember precisely where but I do recall that I was quite overwhelmed by the marvellous, happy, spiritualist people I met. They even presented me with a little gift of African oak, shaped like clasped hands. The idea is that you rub it whenever you feel a bit uptight and it takes away the stress.

'I suppose I went along to that meeting because I had a longstanding interest in spiritualism. I once read a book by a priest who was in contact with another dead priest. The latter described what life was like in the spirit world. It fascinated me so, when Keith's invitation came along, it seemed a good opportunity once again to revive the curiosity I have about life after death.

'According to the spirit priest, everybody in the spirit world is about thirty years of age, everyone dresses the same and there is no sex over there. I particularly liked the flowery stuff in this book, where it said that in "Heaven" when you pick up a handful of sand and let it fall through your fingers, it makes a tuneful, tinkling sound. The grass tinkles, too, when you walk on it. There are no such things as sick flowers, or sick anything. Everything is perfection. People can study whatever they want and there are concerts and all kinds of shows to enjoy. I like that because it means I can carry on being a musician or a photographer which is another big interest and pleasure of mine.

'We all have to believe in something so I now believe this is our fate when we leave this life. I definitely believe I am psychic because I have strong feelings about things, which is what intuition is all about, I suppose.

'Keith particularly impressed me because he told me he could see me in a big show. I told him I'd been in big shows with the Shadows in the past, but he said, "No, I see you in another big show with the Shadows." At the time, that didn't seem at all likely.

'Some months later, right out of the blue, I did get to play again with the Shadows and Cliff Richard, at Wembley Stadium. That hadn't even been planned when I spoke to Keith. His clairvoyance was extraordinary and I was very impressed.'

RICKY VALANCE

'Keith put me in touch with my dead father and came up with some quite astounding facts with regard to him, facts only I could have known.

'We met in my dressing room when I was on a concert tour. I was very into spiritualism and that kind of thing so I asked Keith to give me a reading. Keith told me there was the spirit of a gentleman in the room with us and he went on to describe my father who died about eight years ago. What shook me was the kind of detail he was able to produce, such as the fact that my father had been very ill with a chest problem which caused his chest to cave in.

'He was right: my father suffered from spondylitis (inflammation of the vertebrae), so he hit the nail right on the head! Nobody could have known that, other than me.

'He then went on to say that my father knew I had been trying to contact him and that I was constantly thinking about him. Through Keith, my father reassured me that he was with me in spirit most of the time and that many of the ideas which came to me were put into my mind by my dead father. Then came a touch of my father's typical humour; he added that he became very frustrated when I didn't act on his advice!

'When Keith told me that this gentleman kept calling me "boy", I knew it had to be my dad. It was him to a "T". He was an old Welshman – we're all Welsh – and he would often say to me, "Come on boy", or "How are you, boy?"

'Keith told me I was not to worry any more about my father because he was very much alive and well on the other side and that he had a stick, which he used to carry in this life, and which he now carries with him in spirit. Then Keith asked me if my father had a dog in this life. No, he hadn't but he was very keen on animals, especially dogs. It seems he is now surrounded by them.

'I have to admit that I cried with the emotion of finally being convinced that I will meet my father again. I've always believed in a life after death but now I have had proof that it isn't the end of the line when we die. It has alleviated a lot of my worries and given me a great deal of comfort.

'Maybe it is no coincidence that I have always felt that my life has been protected, which was just as well because I have had many brushes with death. I have escaped two serious road crashes and a near drowning incident which happened off Singapore. Even the song "Tell Laura I Love Her" was to do with death, about a guy who got killed in a stock-car race, but it didn't glorify death. For me, its appeal was that it had such a lovely melody.

'Keith is very gifted and a really genuine person. Now I know that when I need to do so I can probably contact my father again through Keith. I like that.'

I hope these two testimonies speak for themselves. Both Jet and Ricky stress the comfort they now enjoy from the proof they have had about the existence of life after death. As Ricky put it, 'This is not the end of the line.'

Many actors are also clairvoyant, so maybe it has something to do with artistic sensitivity. Television soap star Bill Roache, who joined *Coronation Street* on day one, is another psychic sizzler and, for me, a special one because he knows the gift must be taken seriously.

I have had the pleasure of meeting Bill a number of times and have enjoyed some interesting chats with him about life after death, along the lines of how serious-minded people can sensibly explore what lies ahead when we die.

Bill, who at the time played *Coronation Street*'s long-suffering schoolmaster Ken Barlow, invited me to Granada Studios in Manchester to talk about life after death and to give him a psychic reading.

We sat in the relative privacy of his dressing room, amid mirror, bright lights and make-up. It struck me at the time as a strange place to be talking about our belief that we pass on to a different spiritual dimension when we exhale our last breath in this one! But then, Bill has a distinctive sense of humour and a belief in spirit life based on very personal experiences, so he wouldn't care where he discussed such things as long as they were discussed seriously and sensibly.

We did just that. In fact, I was flattered that he thought it would make good television to explore seriously the ability of a proven clairvoyant and the implications of life after death. He said he would want to take part in such a discussion and I told him I would happily be his psychic guinea pig!

I have told Bill he would make a good medium. He is very spiritually aware but, as far as I know, he hasn't even been to a psychic meeting. Certainly, he has never mentioned it, yet I get the feeling he would like to delve into the psychic world much more deeply than his star status will allow. Imagine the interest the press would take if he turned up at one of my psychic evenings in Manchester! Anyway, he has had a basinful over his involvement with the Druids. Now he pursues his interests privately, well out of view of the media. However, he has spoken openly about his grief over the tragic death of his baby daughter Edwina who died from bronchitis aged only nineteen months.

When I was preparing the material for this book and covering the parts concerning my involvement with Bill Roache, I had a vision of Edwina. I could see a little girl and I sensed very strongly that when she was prepared for her funeral a cross was placed in her right hand, although I could not be sure by whom. Bill said he was unaware of this having happened so, clearly, the cross was not placed there by Bill or his wife Sara. So was I wrong or, if Edwina's mother and father were not the ones who put that cross in the baby's hand, maybe it was another member of the family or someone else. I have to say, though, that I am seldom wrong when I receive such powerful visions.

Bill and Sara grieved very deeply over their sad loss, to the point where they felt they might not even be able to cope with the final farewell to their little girl. On the morning of the funeral, Bill had a vision of his own when the spirit of baby Edwina showed herself to him within a spiritual bright light which shone from high up in one corner of his bedroom.

This was Edwina's way of saying to her mother and father, 'Stop grieving for me. I am happy. There is life after death.' Bill and Sara were comforted by this experience and were then able to handle both the funeral, always especially sad when it is that of a child, and Edwina's memory.

'After the vision I felt a great relief flood over me, and from that moment Sara and I began to rebuild our lives,' Bill Roache later commented.

Bill accepts that he is intuitive, which, as he says, is being psychic, but, wisely, he does have reservations about dabbling in the spirit world. He puts it this way: 'I've studied these things and I know there are entities floating around in the ether looking for entry to our world. The trouble with spiritualism is that it opens up to these, and some of the entities aren't benign. You have to be very wary. We're not meant to be working in these areas but the time is coming when serious studies are going to be made and I will be happy to come forward and work with serious people like Keith Charles. He has impressed me, and I know he is a sincere man. I've met some clairvoyants who are quacks and hoaxers. Unfortunately, the genuine ones, like Keith, are few in number.'

Sadly, few people are as aware as Bill Roache about the need to take spiritualism seriously and that they should not treat it as a party trick, using the dangerous ouija board as a 'key' to enter the spirit world. It is all too easy to disturb the mischievous entities which Bill talks about. To help people understand what I mean by this, I say to them, 'You wouldn't leave your front door open, would you? All right, a nice man might walk by and pop his head inside to tell you he was able to let himself in. But another man might also take advantage of an open front door, let himself in – and cause a lot of bother!'

It is no different when I make contact with the spirit world. I have no idea what kind of spirit is going to come along and when one does I make sure it is not intent on mischief!

Guys like magician Paul Daniels can be a bit mischievous, too. On television, before millions of susceptible viewers, he says, 'Clairvoyants will have you believe this but I can do it, too. Isn't it amazing?'

The only difference is that, like all magicians, he does what he does through trickery. I don't use trickery. What I passed on to Ricky Valance, Jet Harris, Bill Roache and many more far from foolish people was information which came to me from spirit. I couldn't manipulate that. Either it was accurate or it was rubbish.

Daniels is, of course, very clever at what he does, but I don't think it reflects very well on him that he is always taking sideswipes at mediums in the same way it would be unreasonable if mediums were always taking swipes at him for producing a brand of entertainment which can sometimes be quite boring. It certainly achieves very little by comparison to the comfort and joy brought to people by many mediums.

The singer Lulu came to one of our meetings, not so much because she was in need of spiritual comfort, but, I'd say, more out of curiosity. There was nothing wrong in that. Her husband John and their son came as well, all three as guests of Derek Robinson, president of Wimbledon Spiritualist Church, where the event took place.

The evening starred Doris Collins and was being filmed for Australian television, so Lulu's presence, and that of several other showbusiness celebrities, added a touch of glamour.

Afterwards, when we were having tea, Lulu said to me, 'Doris is good, isn't she?' Then she asked what I did and I told her I was also a medium. At this point Derek Robinson came over and asked Lulu if she'd mind them having 'a little smudge together'. That's his Cockney way of saying he wanted to have his picture taken with her. Lulu happily obliged.

However, Doris Collins seemed quite put out by this. She later complained to Derek and to me that she didn't think it was right to ask celebrities to pose for pictures. It was taking advantage of their visit. Could it be that Doris was jealous that we had had our picture taken with Lulu? However, the cameras were rolling for an Australian television documentary and Doris Collins was the psychic star turn so perhaps she had some excuse for showing a little artistic temperament.

Lulu is another artist with a definite gift as a healer. It shows in her spiritual aura of mauve and pink. A lot of healing power comes from her and I'd say that underneath that cool, yet bubbly, personality is a person who cares very deeply for faraway problems such as the tragedy of Ethiopia. She would care about homeless people. Perhaps she will care that she could also be a healer and consider developing her gift.

I came across blonde actress Kitty Aldridge when I was making house-to-house inquiries as a policeman. I just knocked on her door and hadn't a clue who she was. As soon as she opened the door, however, I knew we were going to get along well. She has a brilliant aura and showed herself to be a shrewd businesswoman with very strong self-motivation and a sense of purpose.

During our conversation on the doorstep, I mentioned that I was a medium and she immediately said, 'Oh, come on in. My husband would love to have a chat with you.'

I completed my police work with Kitty (star of TV's *Paradise Club*) and her equally well-known film producer husband Neil, then we talked about life after death. Kitty and Neil were especially fascinated that I was a psychic policeman.

Over the next few weeks and months, I spent quite a lot of time with Kitty and Neil at their home. I met other film producer friends of theirs, including Neil's brother Cedric who worked on the American Ninja Turtle film, which he produced.

It's funny how things turn out but our friendship blossomed to such a degree that we all chipped in to buy a greyhound. We called her Wolf Power and raced her. She didn't make us millionaires but she paid for her keep with a number of wins. In fact, she was a finalist in three major races. Ever since I was a boy of twelve, when my grandad took me to the dogs in Brighton, I've loved greyhounds and the atmosphere of the racing stadium.

Kitty would make a good spiritual counsellor and although I don't think it's really the kind of thing she would want to do all the time, she is an excellent listener for anyone with problems.

Both Kitty and Neil came to one of my psychic meetings at Chatham in Kent, out of curiosity not because they are spiritualists or even want to be. They told me they were impressed with the large number of people who were attending a psychic evening for the first time and especially with the large number of younger people present. Kitty presented a cheque to a young lad who had cancer.

We raise a great deal of money for charity in order to help as many people and causes as we can but sometimes it smacks us in the face, like it did when I became involved in raising money for the Ben Hardwick appeal.

The so-called Born Again Christians aren't too charitable towards us either. We have had a number of clashes with these people when they have tried to cause trouble at our meetings, although, I must add, not with Cliff Richard, who is a true Christian. I know he wouldn't support any form of violence or the intolerance shown by some Born Again Christians. Sometimes I wish we had another of our psychic friends along at our more 'lively' meeting places. Paul McKenna, the internationally famous hypnotist, would make a wonderful hypnotic hitman! If any Born Again Christians infiltrated one of our meetings and began to disrupt it, Paul would shut them up quicker than anybody. He would lay them out and we would carry them out!

In fact, Paul is much too gentle a man to be involved in anything so aggressive. I have always been fascinated by his stage presence. Here is a man who really holds an audience and controls it in many more ways than one. He does this with the help of bright, flashing lights, stimulating music and eye-catching clothes. I believe mediums can learn a lesson here.

I am now exploring a way of making my psychic experience evenings something people will never forget, using loud music and laser lighting piercing the auditorium and bouncing off walls. I'll even wear an Alvin Stardust suit if it creates a lasting impression, with people going home at the end of the show feeling they've had a wonderful night out.

I know I can get the psychic bit right, now I want to bring the presentation upmarket. Unfortunately, spiritualism is still presented, and still looked upon, as though it comes from the dark ages.

Astrologer Russell Grant is very spiritual. One of these days, when I meet him, we must talk about it, because I have no doubt that astrologers with a psychic back-up are so much more powerful in their predictions, as in the case of Russell.

Somewhere along the line, Derek Robinson introduced me to a lady named Jackie Evans who worked for a management company. She came along to see me in action at a meeting in Tunbridge Wells, the idea being that her company would include me in some thirty shows around Britain and promote me as a medium. Russell Grant was also on this company's books.

Then, unfortunately, I was very unwell and was stuck in bed for a number of days. Out of the blue

Russell Grant rang. We had a brief chat on the phone and he wished me a speedy recovery. We agreed it would be nice to meet up but we never did. Not long after, Jackie left the company that brought us together and started her own.

Russell has been to Wimbledon Spiritualist Church but I don't think he makes too much of his spiritual interests. As I say, the public can be a bit fickle and if you are in the public eye it is not always in your best interests to be seen to be involved in something which many would regard as a fringe religion. They run a mile.

When it comes to running, however, at one time no man anywhere in the world could run faster than Carl Lewis. He covered the track with the speed of greased lightning.

It was around 1984. Carl had just returned from the Olympics with four gold medals and I caught up with him at the Westmorland Hotel in London, as a policeman rather than as a medium. The manager had called me to the hotel to check it over and to show Carl Lewis that there was a police presence around. I was introduced to Carl. It was nearly 10 a.m. and Carl was having a leisurely breakfast when I turned up. I was invited to sit down and join him.

We spent a very pleasant hour talking about athletics but I couldn't help picking up feelings that here was a man carrying a lot of spiritual anger, a man who didn't seem to know where he was going or what was expected of him – other than to run fast. I was frustrated in that I really felt I could have helped with some psychic healing and yet it wouldn't have been right for me to try to do so. Imagine the reaction if I'd suddenly blurted out, 'Hi, Carl. I'm psychic and I can help you with some healing!' I don't think I'd have seen him for dust! In fact, he'd have probably broken another speed record making his escape!

The words 'spiritualist' and 'spiritualism' conjure up pictures in many people's minds of little old ladies linking hands round a table and calling up the dead. Sadly, I sometimes think that in tarring myself with the brush of spiritualist I am limiting my opportunities to create a wider public interest in the psychic. On the other hand, if I described myself as a Born Again Christian with a terrific psychic ability, that would be readily acceptable.

Perhaps this was my problem with Carl Lewis. Knowing that I was a spiritualist as well as a policeman, it is possible he found it difficult to open up to me on a spiritual level.

CHAPTER FIVE

NIGHTMARE OVER BABY BEN

The date 4 August 1985 is etched on my mind as if it was the day war broke out. On a personal level, I suppose this was the day my own war erupted when a national newspaper published a story about me with the headline: 'Baby Ben – tragic mum's anger at psychic cop's "message"'.

For a man who has never believed in the existence of any kind of spiritual hell, I would say the torment I went through over my well-intentioned, but obviously misconstrued, involvement in the Baby Ben story was my own personal hell on earth.

Brave little Ben Hardwick captured the hearts of Britain when Esther Rantzen told the story on her television show *That's Life* of him being the youngest child in Europe to have a liver transplant.

Moved by the story of Ben's fight for a normal life, the nation dipped deep into its pockets to help this incredibly brave little boy. Over £250,000 was raised and used by the Addenbrooke Hospital, in Cambridge, where Ben had his operation, to provide a fully equipped Ben Hardwick Room to help other children in need of a similar transplant operation.

Here was a smashing little kid who was going to die unless he had a transplant. I was deeply moved like everyone else. Ben received his new liver on 21 January 1983, bringing him a new chance of life, but tragically, after a second operation in 1985, he died aged two. Despite the success of his liver transplant, the strain of the second operation was too much and his tiny heart stopped.

I mourned his death along with the rest of the country and our hearts went out to his mother Debbie and father Billy. In fact, my involvement with the family was on something of a personal level. I had known Billy Hardwick, Ben's dad, for twelve years. I knew about Billy's background and how he'd grown up on a council estate, one of thirteen brothers and sisters. It was not the best of circumstances.

I also knew him while his little son Ben was dying of an incurable and rare liver disease. I knew that, despite Billy's many disadvantages in life, he was a kind, loving and caring father who really did deserve a second chance to make good of his life.

Then, one evening after work, as I was driving along the A3 on my way home to Chessington in Surrey, a most extraordinary thing happened to me.

I was at the wheel of my car, not thinking of anything in particular, and certainly not, at that moment, thinking about Ben. I just wanted to get home and unwind. Quite suddenly, I became very aware of spirit around me. When this happens I get a tingly feeling, rather like pins and needles. I did as I always do in this situation. I asked out loud: 'Who is it?' in the same way that, when someone knocks on your door, you go to the door and ask, 'Who is it?'

The voice in my head just kept repeating: 'Talk to Billy Hardwick.' I had no idea who the message was from in the spirit world, nor did the voice tell me.

To be frank, I didn't really take too much notice. This kind of thing happens quite often; it is nothing particularly sensational to a medium. Spirit voices can come to me anywhere, at any time. Sometimes it is significant, at other times it is not.

This time it was to be especially significant and the events that followed resulted in a full-blown police investigation that could have finished in me being unceremoniously kicked out of the police force if there had been any doubt about my integrity and innocent involvement in the drama that ensued.

Had I really heard this voice, had I imagined it? I couldn't be sure. My concentration went back to the radio and the build-up of traffic as I neared Chessington.

Three miles further along the road, I turned left at the Ace of Spades and there, outside the restaurant, I suddenly spotted Billy Hardwick. It was unbelievable. In the usual way I'd only ever see him two or three times a year, yet, out of the blue he was there in front of me only minutes after spirit had given me his name.

As I say, I wasn't a close friend of his. I just knew him through my work and because he lived in the same locality. We were on nodding terms.

I stopped my car and felt compelled to go back and speak to him. 'Hello, Billy,' I called out, as I drew alongside him on the pavement.

'Hello, Mr Wright,' responded Billy.

'I need to have a quick word with you. Is that all right?' I asked.

'Of course it is. What's on your mind?'

I had second thoughts about discussing with him, there and then, what I had just experienced driving along in my car. It didn't seem the right place or the right moment, so I asked Billy if he'd like to come to my house. People who know me get used to my strange messages and Billy agreed.

When he turned up, as arranged, a few days later,

he was with a woman. I told him that I was a copper but that I wanted to see him because of my other work as a clairvoyant.

We sat in my living room having a cup of tea, letting the conversation flow naturally and talking about the spirit message I'd received two evenings earlier in my car. Billy was surprised and I am not sure he really believed me. Then, as we sat chatting, Ben came through from spirit.

'I want to talk to my daddy,' Ben said to me.

I told Billy that I had Ben with me and he looked at me, still not quite sure what was going on. Ben knew that his father needed positive proof it was really him and began to tell me things that only his father would know.

He told me about his teddy, named Fudge, and about a £50 note he had been given on his birthday just before he died. Ben had been to see one of his uncles and this uncle had handed Ben the £50 note. Ben couldn't hold the money so his uncle handed the note to him tucked in a cup. Only a few members of the family knew this.

'Is he all right?' Billy asked me.

Ben answered: 'Tell Daddy I'm happy here. It's very nice. Sue is looking after me.'

I didn't know who Sue was but Billy told me that Sue was his mum, who had died two years before, of cancer.

I knew that Billy was not a religious lad and had

never been interested in spiritualism but I could see that mentioning his mum's name and the story of the £50 note had really made him take seriously what was happening and what Ben was saying through me.

Ben told me many intimate and special things so that his father would know it could only be him talking to me. As Ben continued, his little voice became clearer and stronger. Ben even told me that, in spirit, he had met Matthew Fewkes, who was the donor for his liver. It was a very moving moment for Billy and for me.

Billy told me: 'Keith, I've been so unhappy since Ben's death. He was the best thing in my life and I loved him so much.'

I know it helped Billy a lot my being a link between him and Ben. It gave Billy a great deal of comfort to know that the spirit of his son is always with him and that, although Ben has passed from this life, he is happy and well cared for in the next.

Billy said he was very concerned that if money wasn't forthcoming for these very expensive transplant operations, the hospital transplant unit might have to close down. As a result, Billy said he wanted to help to raise money to stop this happening. I thought I might be able to help. I knew former newspaperman Derek Jameson, who is currently a radio presenter. Ellen Petrie, his other half, was a reporter on the *Daily Star* at the time. I invited them and Billy round to my home for dinner.

The idea was to get the three of them together to see if they could help Billy with his fund-raising aims. Other well-known names came to mind too. Billy said he knew snooker professional Jimmy White, so there was another possible fund-raising outlet.

I felt I could also contribute by producing brochures and selling them at £1 a time at my nationwide clairvoyance meetings. I would pay for the brochures and any money made from the sales would go to the appeal. Billy was pleased with this suggestion. He provided photographs and wrote a letter which went into the centrefold.

I went off on tour with my tour organiser Derek Robinson. At each meeting, in various parts of Britain, I made it quite clear that these brochures were a bit special because the £1 a time they raised was going to the Baby Ben Appeal.

Everything went fine until 1 August 1985 when we reached the Institute of Leith in Fife. Other venues were in Edinburgh and Glasgow but the Leith meeting was very poorly attended, with only about forty people present. We were required to close our meeting by 9.30 p.m. and be out of the hall by 10 p.m.

Just before the end of the meeting, Derek was at the back, ready to sell more brochures as the people left for home, when a young woman walked in and just helped herself to one of the brochures, thinking they were free. Derek told her they cost £1 and took her money.

We were curious about her because she had not attended our psychic evening, so when she approached me in my dressing room and said she wanted to ask me a few questions, it struck me as a bit odd.

By this time, the caretaker was impatiently hurrying us along and my stomach was rumbling with hunger. I was ready to sink a plateful of fish and chips. I asked the girl if she knew of a place where we could eat; if so, she could ask me her questions there. She said she knew of a restaurant so Derek and I followed in our car as she drove through Leith. We were too late, however, and the chippy had just closed, so we all piled into the pub next door. As we settled with our drinks, the girl then asked what I thought about life after death.

It wasn't earth-shattering; many people ask me that question. I was still none the wiser about the girl's motives, though. I thought she was just someone curious about spiritualism. I hadn't guessed what she was really up to but I soon found out.

As calm as you like, she suddenly announced: 'I will tell you why I am here. I am from the *Sunday Mirror* and I must tell you we are exposing you in the paper tomorrow as a fraud.' She added that Debbie Hardwick, Ben's mother, had complained to them that I was a fraud.

I was so shocked I nearly burst into tears. In a matter of seconds the bottom seemed to have dropped out of my world. All kinds of thoughts came rushing into my head, such as the fact that I was on holiday from my work as a policeman and seven hundred miles away from my wife and family. How would they take it when they suddenly read in next day's Sunday paper that I was branded as a fraud and a charlatan? It was even too late to put through a call and try to explain what was happening.

To cap it all, Derek and I couldn't find digs that night so, on our way to our next meeting in Glasgow, we parked our car on the banks of Loch Lomond and slept there!

Sure enough, one of the national Sunday papers carried the story about me on page two under the huge headline: 'Baby Ben — tragic mum's anger at psychic cop's "message"'.

In essence the article accused me of making money out of Ben by publishing the fact that I had received spirit messages from him and by selling the brochures at £1 a time. There was no mention of the fact that the money was all going to the Baby Ben Appeal Fund and only the briefest mention in the story that Billy's own testimony was included in the brochure.

The furore this caused caught up with me in Glasgow when Derek and I arrived that Sunday evening. About a hundred people were in the audience, waiting for me to give out my psychic messages, and the church president was in a state of panic over the press interest in me. 'Thank goodness you are here. We've had reporters kicking on the doors since 6.30 this morning. What have you done?' he asked.

I told him I had done nothing and then showed him a copy of the report in the paper, which carried no mention of the fact that I'd told their reporter about all the brochure money going to the Baby Ben Memorial Appeal Fund.

The paper also carried a highly emotive picture and caption which read: 'Devoted – Debbie with brave, dying Ben'. I got very upset about it all.

I missed the reporters who had apparently been trying to catch up with me all day, but I did explain to the large audience that I had done nothing wrong and that the story in the brochure was printed with the full approval and backing of Billy Hardwick for the benefit of the Baby Ben Appeal. They understood and accepted my explanation. We had a very good meeting that night.

However repercussions were now following on. The next morning, Monday, I phoned my wife Maureen to tell her what had happened, only to learn from her that she had already read in that morning's paper that I had been suspended from my work as a policeman.

Maureen had only picked up the story when she went to buy her newspaper from our local newsagent in Brighton. 'Here, seen what they are saying about Keith?' he asked Maureen. She hadn't and was devastated, yet there was no way she could contact me. She had to wait until I contacted her on the Monday.

The story followed me down to the south-coast resort of Hove where I had my next meeting. More explanations, only this time the audience applauded me. I was able to tell them that I had checked with the police as to whether the newspaper story reporting my suspension was true and that it wasn't. I was still a fully active detective constable with the Metropolitan police. However, my department did receive a two-page-long, official complaint about me from Debbie Hardwick, along the lines of the Sunday paper's accusations.

Of course, the police conducted their own internal investigation to be sure my psychic interest had been recorded as an 'outside interest', which it had, and that I was not fraudulently raising money for my own benefit, as the newspaper story seemed to imply.

We had a thousand brochures printed and we sold all of them at £1 each, raising £1,000. The brochures cost 60p each to produce, and Derek Robinson, who handled the cash raised, gave £405 (for which we have a letter of receipt) to the Baby Ben Memorial Appeal. Sadly, it was a little short of the £500 I had hoped to raise.

Appropriately enough, the £405 was accepted on behalf of the Baby Ben Appeal by sixties singer Billy J. Kramer who made famous the song 'Little Children'. He came along to one of our dinner dances and sang a couple of songs as I recall. I also gave him a psychic reading.

So, that was what happened to the money we raised but, as a result of the complaint, I had to face a police interview over the affair and I have to say I didn't much like the tone of this interview. Even though I knew I was innocent of the charges against me, I felt most uncomfortable. I now know how some people must have felt when I was on the other side of the table, as a police officer, interviewing them.

Other people named in the brochure were interviewed, including tour organiser Derek Robinson, right through to the printer.

I heard a rumour that Bill Roache was unhappy about his picture being included in the brochure but when I next saw him, at the Border television studios in Carlisle, he said he was not worried about it.

After that I had to wait about ten months for the police investigation report into the complaint against me. Hanging in the balance was my whole future and sixteen years' service in the police force, including my pension rights.

At home, my wife was being pointed at in the street and my kids mercilessly teased at school about their 'nutty father'. It was not a very nice time for any of us. It seemed so unfair to me because all I had wanted to do was help Billy and Ben's memorial appeal.

I have no regrets over my involvement with Ben

Hardwick. I am a great believer in life plans. We wouldn't learn anything if we knew what was going to happen. All I was aware of was the fact that I had had communication with a spirit child who said he wanted to speak to his dad. As to the name of the child, it made no difference. I had simply been chosen as the link.

I never did meet Debbie Hardwick but I did tell the senior police officers who investigated me that I would be happy to meet and talk to her about her accusations. From her attitude, however, it was clear that she had no intention of meeting me. I have no axe to grind with Debbie Hardwick. In fact, I felt very sorry for her because she went through a very difficult time, as did her husband Billy. I happen to believe I was chosen by spirit to pass on Ben's messages to his father because of my direct link to him, because I knew Billy. What happened subsequently, concerning the police investigation, was not caused by spirit but by Mrs Hardwick and the police themselves.

Some people have said, 'Ah, spirit caused all that,' but this was not true. The only other comment I would make is that I would have liked to have been more prepared for the police investigation but I have no regrets that it happened.

At work, my colleagues treated me as normal and I think most of them, like most of my friends, only felt sympathy. This was a big comfort.

Eventually, the police complaint investigation

report came through. To my great relief, no disciplinary action was taken.

The ten months' wait, however, had been horrific. To add to the pressure on me during this time, I was also investigated by the Inland Revenue, so the tax man moved in on me just as the Baby Ben police investigation ended.

The two investigations were linked because, as the tax man told me, it had come to his notice that I had been earning extra money – and where was his bit?

All of this has made me think very seriously about undertaking any similar charity appeals. I would not want to go through all that hassle again, knowing I had done nothing wrong but needing to prove it because of a biased complaint and a biased newspaper report.

CHAPTER SIX

MY VISION OF
LUCAN'S DEATH

Sometimes it is difficult to be both a policeman and a medium as I found out when I had a spirit-inspired vision about the death of Lord Lucan, the well-known gambler who was wanted for the murder of his children's nanny twenty years ago.

Even today, nobody knows officially whether Lucan is dead or alive, although there have been unsubstantiated sightings of him in a number of places abroad. Unofficially, I know he is dead.

I had a vision about his fate one afternoon when I was at home with my ex-wife Maureen. I was sitting at our dining room table, relaxing after coming off night shift. It had been a hard night's work and I was feeling quite tired out but I know I was not asleep or even dozing. I was fully aware of my surroundings and what I could 'see'.

For no real reason that I can recall, I suddenly became aware of what I suppose most people would call their 'mind's eye' looking in on a country scene, with the name Lucan and a place called Uckfield ringing through my head. It wasn't being shouted by anyone but was sort of 'echoing' inside my head.

I didn't seem to have any control over what I was seeing but I knew this was no ordinary dream experience. If anything, suddenly finding myself looking at this strange scene made me extra alert. I called out to Maureen to come in and to bring me a pencil and paper. Of course, she hadn't a clue what was happening but when she saw my trance-like gaze, she realised at once because it had happened to me before.

I began to draw.

Curious about this brilliantly clear vision, I decided to drive to Uckfield unofficially to check the scene of the murder as I had seen it.

My sketch showed a large house standing on a hilltop and a large expanse of lawn running down the hillside away from the big house. At the foot of the grassy slope I 'saw' a body sprawled, face down, alongside what I can only describe as a large concrete drain – a section of what I think are called storm sewers.

A man was standing with legs apart at the top of the lawn, near the house, a smoking shotgun in his hands, looking down the grassy slope at the body. He was wearing plus-fours, and a tweed jacket and trousers. He was smartly dressed, like a gamekeeper.

The Lucan incident was before my time as a fully trained detective. It occurred at Lucan's Belgravia home in London in November 1974, when I'd only been in the police force for five years.

The last positive sighting of Lucan was at a friend's house in Uckfield. This was where Lucan had gone after the murder of the nanny, so I drove to Grants Hill House, in Uckfield, the home of thirty-nine-year-old Ian Maxwell-Scott, a gambling friend of Lucan and cousin to the Duke of Norfolk. It was known that Lucan had driven to see the Maxwell-Scotts, presumably for comfort, advice and as a bolt-hole while he collected his thoughts and decided what to do next.

According to a newspaper report at the time, 'He arrived alone at the house in Church Street, just off Uckfield High Street and stayed two hours. Mr Maxwell-Scott was not at home.'

The report went on to say, 'Mr Maxwell-Scott's thirty-eight-year-old wife, Susan, mother of six, told of Lord Lucan's visit. She said, "I was alone except for two of the children who were asleep upstairs. My husband was in London and I was rather surprised at Lord Lucan's arrival. It was about 11.30 p.m. He came in. We had a long talk. He sat down and wrote two letters to Mr Shand-Kydd, his brother-in-law. He stayed for about two hours, leaving at about 1.30 a.m. on Friday morning. He said that he did not wish for a meal." '

Mrs Maxwell-Scott said Lord Lucan drove off in a car but she told police she was unable to describe the vehicle. Lucan was never seen again.

I have to admit that the vision and the sketches I made were eerie. I discovered that Grants Hill House was no longer there. The Maxwell-Scotts had sold up and moved away and the old house was demolished to make way for a complex of old people's homes.

When I arrived at the site of the old house, I was puzzled because my sketch seemed to be wrong in one rather important detail. The housekeeper in the old people's home, who remembered the old house, explained precisely where it had stood. Sure enough one very tall tree, which would have been alongside one end of the old house, was still standing. But where was the tree that would have stood the other end? There wasn't one. 'There used to be but it was blown down in the October 1987 hurricane,' explained the housekeeper, apparently puzzled by so much interest in a missing tree.

I then stood on the lawns which are still there and

which once dropped away down the hill from the back of the old house. Where the grounds ended at the foot of the steep slope, and where I had indicated I had seen Lucan's body sprawled on the ground alongside what appeared to me to be a huge concrete drain, was a housing estate.

Further checks at the local police station and with local residents established the fact that the housing estate was in the course of construction just about the time Lucan went missing, so it was quite probable that storm drains had been on the ground where I had seen them in my vision.

There is no way I can say who I had also 'seen' standing on the top of the hill with the smoking gun in his hands. I have no idea if the previous owners even employed a gamekeeper or allowed one in their grounds.

So, is the body of Lord Lucan buried under the storm drains on this Uckfield housing estate? Was he shot by accident, or even deliberately?

One man who knew the owners of Grants Hill House well enough to be paying regular visits to the house at the time of Lucan's disappearance, was a local trader who, in more recent years, had become a traffic warden. He told me that he had heard most theories about Lucan's mysterious disappearance – other than mine which he considered the most bizarre and yet perhaps the most credible. If Lucan had been murdered, what better place to dump him than in the deep footings, later covered by heavy storm drains, underneath a housing estate! There is no way anyone is going to dig up a housing estate in order to try to trace a body which might have been buried there some twenty years before. It would be almost the perfect murder!

As for the motive for killing him, I can only make a guess. As I have said, he could have been mistaken for an intruder and shot, then when it was discovered who he was and what he was believed to have done, his disposal in this way was probably the easiest and safest solution. If you want me to offer a still more bizarre answer, perhaps it was Lucan's own wish that he should die at the hands of his mystery killer. Did he ask to be shot? Did he even shoot himself and stagger down that grassy slope? Maybe the man in my vision holding the smoking gun was Lucan himself, a moment before he died by his own hand? The man was clearly in a distraught mental state, with little future ahead of him, only a lifetime on the run from the police. Of course, this is all speculation. In all probability, the truth will never, ever be known.

I have never put forward my psychic theories about the fate of Lucan to my bosses. If, ultimately, I cannot prove what I believe to be true, how can I expect the police investigating Lucan's disappearance to take my theories and vision seriously? Obviously, I cannot.

People seem to think that with my connections to the spirit world I should be the best detective in

Britain, if not in the world! 'How can you go wrong?' they ask. 'You're a good clairvoyant so all you do is call up your friends "over there" and ask them to point you in the right direction. They know every-thing so all they have to do is drop a name and address, perhaps even a telephone number, into your head, and you go and get your man. Easy!'

It would be wonderful if it was so simple but, unfortunately, it is not. First of all, those spirits 'over there' are not fountains of all knowledge, able to predict or reveal everything that is going on in our world. In the same way very few people who watch the popular television programme *Crime Watch* will be able to help the policemen in the studio to solve the problems they have screened. Certainly, a number will recognise someone or have a family link and may choose to phone and tell a researcher or policeman an important name or some relevant details about the case concerned.

The same goes for spirit. Quite often they do help me in my work as a London police detective but I don't think my guv'nor would be too happy if I told him I knew who committed a certain murder because one of my spirit friends had told me so! In the police force we only deal in hard evidence gleaned from this world, not tip-offs which come through to spiritual-ists like me from the world of spirit.

To some people that will sound very convenient, but it is not a question of convenience, it is the way mediums work, and the way the law demands detection is carried out.

Having said that, my own police work has been helped on numerous occasions by my clairvoyance. Writer Mike Winters, the former comedian who partnered his brother Bernie, will testify to that.

I went to a West London hotel where a robbery had been reported only to find that the victim was the celebrity Mike Winters. As soon as I entered his room, I had some very strong and specific feelings about the robbery and what had, and had not, been stolen.

Almost before I had introduced myself, Mike, who is now a full-time writer and lives in Miami, led me into his sitting room and I stood there for a few moments, just turning slowly on my heels, absorbing the strong vibes I could feel flowing through me.

Mike looked a bit puzzled, then asked, 'What is it?' perhaps thinking I was doing my Sherlock Holmes bit and was about to come up with some stunning solution! I don't know about stunning but I think Mike was quite surprised when I explained. I told him that apart from being a copper, I was also a clairvoyant and that, for some strange reason, I was picking up very strong vibes about the robbery.

Mike seemed to be especially fascinated but I wasn't quite sure why until later, when he revealed that his next book was to be about a medium who solves a case of rape using his psychic powers! 'So what do you feel about this one, then?' asked Mike, egging me on with a partly personal and partly professional interest.

'I can tell you that your wife won't be seeing her jewellery again, apart from one very special piece,' I told him. I was right, too. That one special piece was his wife's antique gold watch and it had been well out of the thief's reach when he paid his most unwelcome visit.

'I took it to the jewellers to have it cleaned only this morning, before the thief broke in,' explained Mike, still clearly upset by his wife's loss.

Mike Winters told me he'd been very impressed by my revelations, which also included a description of the criminal. He commented that I was the one who should be investigated so that more could be discovered about clairvoyance!

The incident, and my own psychic involvement in it, found its way into the newspapers. Mike told one writer: 'I became fascinated with Keith's dual life, a policeman by day and a medium by night. That is why, in my book *Razor Sharp*, I had the main character use a psychic to solve a rape case.'

He said about me, 'I don't know that I accept all that Keith believes but there is no doubt that he does have unusual and amazing psychic gifts. I think his unique and mystical talent should be investigated because it could be instrumental in opening up a new vista of thought and understanding about life and what he calls "the other side".'

I have remained friends with Mike Winters ever since. We exchange Christmas cards and if he is in London, with a bit of free time on his hands, he is quite likely to get in touch.

Mike Winters has kindly said of me: 'I suppose I hadn't given much thought to the possibility of there being life after death but that all changed from 1989 onwards when I lost so many dear people, including my brother Bernie, my brother-in-law, my sister-in-law, my mother-in-law and my niece, as well as some dear friends from showbusiness: Dickie Henderson and Matt Monro.

'These tragedies preyed on my mind so it was good to have Keith giving me some spiritual warmth and sympathy. When the finality of death hits you on such a personal level, many questions tend to flood into your mind. I was no exception. As a writer, I am fully aware of the need to question all things around me.

'Keith is a new breed of psychic and, being a police officer, is skilled at asking questions. He is especially suited to the task of bringing more understanding about our fate or, rather, the fate of our souls, when we have come to the end of our earthly existence.

'Our understanding of life, although still minimal, has probably never been greater and, as we move into the twenty-first century, our understanding of the possibility of a form of life after death must be even more seriously considered. Whether you believe in life after death or not is probably academic. The fact is that, until it can be finally proved, it cannot be acceptably disproved!

'Keith takes a refreshingly new look at this whole uncharted area of human understanding. He is not afraid to criticise and accuse where he believes it right to do so. With him there are no shadowy seances; no dark rooms where sleight of hand can be used to cheat. Keith Charles is light open air – straight on.

'Coming from the world of showbusiness, I find his revelations especially fascinating. Maybe, as Keith suggests, people with an artistic temperament have that psychic edge over the rest of us. It all helps towards a greater understanding of one of the mysteries that is as old as life itself – what really happens when our lives on earth finally expire? I believe Keith has a good many of the answers.'

Many psychics are quickly on the telephone to the police, or to newspapers, with their visions, their spirit information and the like. In most cases these so-called psychics are not psychics at all but just well-meaning people who 'have a feeling' about something or just like the idea of getting police attention. I have had experience of this kind of public interest myself when I've been involved in crime detection.

In the police, we take any information seriously because you can never be sure where some fragment of a clue, or lead, may come from. There was a time when mediums were regarded by the police as mostly a nuisance and those who offered such information were not taken too seriously. That attitude has now changed drastically. The police are much more open-minded about all information given to them in good faith by mediums or anyone else.

I have only come across one senior police officer (now retired) who told me point-blank that my psychic gift was a load of rubbish. He was upset when he overheard me at work talking to a civilian girl typist.

In fact, we were chatting about her brother-in-law, a well-known professional boxer whom I wanted to meet, but this particular Chief Inspector decided it was a good enough excuse for him to have a real go at me over my spiritualist beliefs.

He stormed into our office and, in front of the typist, he accused me of discussing my psychic work with the girl, saying I was trying to turn her head. Turn her head? She was in her mid-twenties, not a young apprentice of sixteen. I just saw red and decided that, senior officer or not, I must have it out with this man. For some reason he was clearly troubled by anything to do with the psychic world and I was just a scapegoat for this inner fear of his. He was totally out of order having a go at me, so I followed him to his office and respectfully told him he owed me an apology.

'No I don't,' he snapped back. He again repeated

that I had been discussing spiritualism and that he would not tolerate me bringing my outside interests into his office.

Again, I repeated that I had not been discussing spiritualism but the girl's professional boxer brother-in-law. He still wouldn't believe me so I called Elaine over. 'Tell the guv'nor what we were discussing,' I asked her.

'Boxing,' said Elaine.

By this time, things had begun to get a bit heavy. My guv'nor ordered Elaine and me out of his office – or he'd throw us out! This was now bullying and I felt he was being very vindictive. Elaine went but I stayed in the guv'nor's room to continue arguing my point. Our raised voices, I was to learn later, were heard in the rest of the office.

The next day, an old boy, an ex-copper, told some of the girl typists about this almighty row he'd heard in the guv'nor's office. Lots of shouting and swearing, he told them. Being a bit deaf, and excited by what he'd heard the day before, his blow-by-blow account of the incident got louder and louder. He didn't know I was the one who had been involved in the argument but as I was listening to what he had to say, the guv'nor himself came along.

The old fella was jabbering on, 'And this guy was telling the guv'nor where to go.' The girls saw the guv'nor approaching and tried hard to hush him up but he carried on with his graphic description of our row. In the end, and with the guv'nor now standing alongside me listening to the old chap's account, I had to come clean. 'It was me and the guv'nor, having the row, wasn't it, guv'nor?'

He just smiled and said, 'Yes'. Then he moved off, our disagreement obviously forgotten.

I don't think I'd have had much chance of converting my ex-guv'nor to spiritualism but I do know a good number of my police colleagues have seen my public demonstrations.

It's just a curiosity about what I do when I am not being a copper. There is no way, though, that I would deliberately try to recruit my colleagues into spiritualism. If they are sufficiently interested to ask me about the psychic world, then I am happy to tell them and to try to answer their questions.

However, policemen tend to be cynical. They want everything spelled out to them. I would hate to have to put on one of my demonstrations of clairvoyance in front of an audience of coppers. So far that has not happened! The nearest I've come is giving my colleagues colour readings when things have been a bit quiet in the office. Briefly this is my ability to tell people about themselves and their future by the colours they give me.

One thing about being a detective and a spiritualist is that each is a good training for the other. As a detective, I am mostly on a hiding to nothing with the public, just as I am as a spiritualist. The general public

Top: Three day police cadet expedition to Wales during 1968. The only memorable experience of the trip was a foul tomato soup and prune breakfast! (I'm second from the left).

Above: One of the perks of the job – (left) helping lost tourists at Trafalgar Square on a summer's day in 1970.

Top: Sharing a joke during Mike Winters' burglary investigation in 1981.

Above: Mike and I became close friends during the investigation. He subsequently invited me to the launch of his book 'Razor Sharp' where I met Peter Stringfellow, who was fascinated by my work.

Top: William Roache and I relaxing after a 'clairvoyant' session at the Granada TV studios in Manchester in 1984.

Above: Esther Rantzen and baby Ben in 1985 at the Addenbrooke's Hospital, Cambs.

Top: Discussing fund-raising ideas for baby Ben with Derek Jameson.

Above: Gordon Higginson – former President of the Spiritualist National Union. In my opinion he was the 'King Of The Mediums'.

Opposite: 'Little Children' singer Billy J. Kramer who was presented with the cheque I had raised on behalf of the baby Ben appeal.

Top: My lovely boys – Michael, Mathew and Daniel.

Above: A day off-duty in Brighton.

Above: Paul McKenna, Ricky Valance, Derek Robinson, my son Mathew and international runner Linda Keogh after a cancer fund-raising event.

Opposite top: Leaving the Spiritualist Church after our wedding ceremony in May 1993.

Opposite: Good old Mum and Dad.

Billy J. Kramer

see us both as fair game for their mickey-taking, yet this doesn't bother me.

I came to terms with this public attitude soon after I joined the force and became the butt of silly jokes from certain sections of the public. Mostly, they don't intend any malice. It is just their way of handling a situation involving a police officer, with which they are not always comfortable. I have found that the situation that works wonders is to make them feel comfortable.

It's precisely the same with spiritualism. People take the mickey out of spiritualism, life after death and mediumship, because it is not something they understand. They are out of their depth, so they have to cover up their ignorance by making fun of it.

Take offence, get angry and become abusive and you have shown up your vulnerability. Show them you can share their fun at your own expense or give them an equally cheeky response and they feel comfortable with your authority or your knowledge which, at this level, exceeds theirs.

As a detective, I have considerable powers of authority invested in me so that I can do my duty in the public's service. As a spiritualist, I am on 'the other side of the counter', so to speak, just another member of the public, with no authority other than my ability to communicate with souls in the spirit world.

I don't mean to sound clever or pompous about

this but, in my police work, both ordinary members of the public and criminals often tell me that I am not like a normal copper because they find they can relate to me! Yet I am not an exception. Many of the policemen I work with are compassionate people; it is just that the public tend to have an image of policemen as people they cannot easily relate to.

We don't make people break the law. We don't make them drive through red traffic lights, park on double yellow lines, or steal from people's homes. When they do these things and get caught, then have a go at us for nicking them, it is their anger with themselves showing itself.

Being a policeman has taught me how to assess people in all kinds of different situations. I have been in situations where customers won't leave a pub when asked by the landlord to go. Say, 'Come on lads, you've had a nice drink. Time to go home now . . .' and, as often as not, when asked in this way, they will move off.

Another time it might be necessary to tell them that if they aren't off the premises in five minutes they will be arrested! However, say that to the wrong group of people and the next thing you know is that you've got about eight blokes kicking seven bells out of you and you'll be lying on the floor wishing you'd said what you needed to say another way! I have had that happen to me.

When comedian Jim Davidson was doing the

summer seaside shows and making people laugh with his police stories and his famous 'nick, nick' catch-phrase, I was on foot patrol in Hastings.

One particular Saturday night, around 11 p.m. and with the town bursting at the seams with holiday-makers, I came across a group of about ten guys who'd just spilled out of a pub very much the worse for too much lager. As I came by in my uniform, they started calling out, 'Nick, nick' and 'Hey, there's old Bill'.

I just looked back at them, smiled and said, 'Yeah, did you see him [Jim Davidson] on TV?' 'Yeah, terrific. Good bloke.' The 'nick, nick' banter continued for a bit but in fun.

'See yer, mate,' I said as I walked on.

'Yeah, night officer,' said one. They moved off without any trouble. The steam had been taken out of what could have been a tricky situation if I'd got too heavy.

Everyone takes the mickey out of policemen so they get used to it and mostly they don't take it too seriously. We are the butt of jokes, whether it's Jim Davidson making them or a guy entertaining his mates over a pint down at the working men's club. It has never bothered me.

Quite a few coppers take the mickey out of me over my work as a psychic but that does not bother me either. I feel I have been selected for my work both as a policeman and as a spiritualist. The qualities I know

I possess, and which enable me to handle both of these areas of my life effectively, make me very aware, and therefore very conscious, of having been selected. I have great compassion and a burning need always to be honest with myself and others, both in my police work and when I am on stage giving public demonstrations of clairvoyance.

I never needed compassion more than in the Clapham train crash. I was on office duty and my station at Battersea had the task of dealing with it. Half the staff had to go off to the rail crash scene itself where injured people had to be rescued, dead bodies had to be extricated from tangled wreckage and property had to be collected and brought back. I saw the look on the faces of those workers who spent many days in the local mortuary. It put years on them. Their faces went grey with anguish and despair.

I could not help reflecting that it was a bizarre situation for me.

In the more usual way, people from the spirit world come to me to make contact with the living here on Earth. At a disaster like that, I found myself involved with those dead casualties who were moving on to the spirit world.

CHAPTER SEVEN

CASE HISTORIES

The little girl's voice was clear. She was telling me she had died in a car crash and that she had come in spirit this evening to say 'thank you' to someone in the audience.

Her words came to me deep inside my head in the same way you might 'think' something a person is saying to you. This is probably the best way I can describe how I 'hear' spirit voices.

As I received the spirit girl's words, I passed them

on to a hushed audience from the stage of the Corn Exchange in the Kent town of Maidstone.

It was a rather damp autumn evening, yet the hall was packed to capacity. People were even standing in the aisles and at the back. The atmosphere was electric as I began to try to locate the right man for this little spirit child.

'His name is Dave, she is telling me,' I continued, my eyes scanning the audience for a raised hand or even a hesitant, raised hand because people are often very nervous, hardly believing that such a message could possibly be for them.

'Come on, Dave, show yourself so I can link you with this little girl . . .' Still no response. People were looking over their shoulders, hoping to see Dave identify himself because they were now bursting with curiosity. They wanted to know what was behind this particular link to spirit, made still more interesting because a child was involved.

'He is at the back,' the spirit girl told me. I had a microphone so I knew I could be heard even at the far end of the hall. In the audience I had a helper with another, cordless microphone so that, when I found Dave, we could all hear his response. But where was Dave!

What I didn't know at the time was that Dave and a woman, who was probably his wife, were sitting some four rows from the back. My journalist friend, Derek, was accompanying me to some meetings as part of his research for this book. At this meeting, unknown to me, he had positioned himself on a gallery alongside the projection room window so that he could look down from behind the audience and observe their reactions.

Long before I discovered bashful Dave, Derek had spotted a woman prodding the man next to her, apparently urging him to stand up and be identified. He kept shaking his head and wouldn't budge.

As I related still more information, just as it was passed on to me by the spirit child, so this woman became more and more frustrated in that the man next to her was the Dave I was trying so hard to find and yet he was apparently too shy to reveal himself.

I continued. The little girl was telling me that Dave had just bought a car and she seemed to be mentioning £400.

I was drawn to a man at the back of the hall and I asked him if his name was Dave. He said it was. 'Have you just bought a car for £400?' No he hadn't, so he was obviously the wrong Dave.

'How will I know it is the right Dave?' I asked the little girl.

'He has a tattoo which shows a heart with a swallow diving through the heart,' she said gently, her 'voice' still coming from deep within my head.

I passed this startling new information to the audience. At this point, the woman in the fourth row from the back almost heaved Dave out of his seat! He was immediately behind the other Dave.

'My name is Dave but it is my second name. My first name is Paul,' he said nervously.

'Ah, thank you, my friend. So you are Dave? Have you just bought a car and do you have this tattoo on your right arm?'

'I bought a car today for £400 and, yes, I do have a tattoo like you described on my right arm.' The audience was spellbound. You could have heard a pin drop; heads were turned to the back.

I was able to tell Dave that he had another tattoo on his left arm which he wanted removed because he didn't like some words on it. He agreed that this was also true.

So, I had obviously found the right Dave, although now his voice was even more subdued. He just could not understand how I knew so much about him.

'This little girl has come back from the spirit world to thank you. Let me tell you how you met. She was about seven and in a car with her mother on her way home on a wet winter's evening when there was an accident. The car left the road, crashed into a tree, instantly killing the mother, then it caught fire. A few moments after the crash you arrived at the scene from the other direction. It was a horrifying sight, with the car starting to burn and the little girl at the window trying to get out . . .'

As the spirit child continued her story, through me, from the stunned look on Dave's face I could see it was precisely the way it had happened. Then tears of emotion flowed as he relived the horror.

'Without hesitation, you lifted the child from the car, cradled her in your arms and sat with her on the roadside as other motorists and the rescue services dealt with the fire and the child's mother. The little girl is telling me that as you cradled her head in your bare arms, one of her last earthly memories was your heart and swallow tattoo. Then, sadly for you, she passed into the spirit world.'

It was too much for Dave to hear and relive. He wept quite openly, comforted by the lady who, as I say, I presumed was his wife. She was also in tears. From the handkerchiefs which suddenly appeared in the dimly lit auditorium, it was clear that quite a few people out there were in tears too.

The little girl asked Dave not to be sad over her death any more. She wanted him to know that she was happy in the spirit world with her mother; and she wanted her rescuer's earthly life to be happy, too.

The audience broke into spontaneous applause at this touching little link with the spirit world.

This was good evidence, the kind of spirit co-operation that makes some of my meetings really buzz with excitement. Yet, I cannot cajole spirit or an audience into creating the right atmosphere. Those who come to my meetings are looking for proof positive that there is life after death. When spirit comes to them, they are satisfied beyond any shadow of doubt that the link is genuine.

I cannot force spirits to come back and communicate. People who go along to my meetings go out of curiosity, because they desperately want to contact a loved one or even just to rubbish the whole idea.

My style of mediumship is probably unique because I like to bring a sense of fun into my contact with both earthly audiences and spirit links. I want none of the mystery and mumbo-jumbo associated with traditional spiritualism so people either like the way I talk to those who have passed on or they don't. It either entertains them or it offends them.

I warm up my audiences just as a comedian will warm up a television studio audience. I welcome them, tell them a few funny stories and probably even joke a bit at the expense of some of those in the audience. If I can get them laughing, feeling relaxed and bring meaningful messages to a number of them, then they will go away after a few hours, having had a wonderful evening. It whets their appetite and they will want to come back for more.

The trouble is that many come to these meetings out of curiosity and just a little afraid they might be picked out for a message. Could they cope with it? If there are a thousand people at a meeting, there is no way I can give out a thousand messages. Perhaps I might manage only ten so these have to be of good quality.

I did my first public demonstration through Derek

Robinson on Friday 9 September 1983 in Kettering. Another medium, named Fred Reynolds, was the star turn.

How well I remember that first occasion when I went on stage and spoke directly to a large public meeting. There was seating for about five hundred in what I think must have been the town hall. There were wooden arches set into the walls and dusty paintings of cavaliers and kings looked down on us. The stage was made of a creaky wooden flooring and there was no public address system.

Not being an actor with a booming voice, and wanting to be sure that my initiation went without a hitch, I borrowed a small, portable, forty-watt amplifier, with a hand-held microphone. Even though I was naturally a bit apprehensive, I was still excited.

By the opening of the meeting, some three hundred faces were looking up at the platform. Fred did his bit. Our promoter, Derek Robinson, tried hard, too, to ensure that there were no problems but we hadn't taken into account the 'walking dead' of Kettering in our audience. They seemed intrigued by what was taking place but showed very little reaction.

I went on at about 8.45 p.m., my usual chirpy self, full of fun and chivvying the audience into some kind of response, even if it was to 'Shut up, and get off!' No such luck. I told one man he drove a white van, to which he said 'Yes'. Then I told him he wanted to sell it, and he said 'No'. I didn't seem to be getting anywhere with any of them.

I'd only been on stage for fifteen minutes, yet people began getting up out of their seats and leaving. A trickle turned into a torrent! I felt absolutely awful and completely to blame for what appeared to me to be my total failure with my first public demo. All right, it had been a struggle, but had I really been so bad?

When the meeting closed, some people from the local spiritualist church came up and told me how much they had enjoyed my demonstration of clairvoyance. I felt they were just being kind, knowing it was my first time, and told them they didn't need to show me their sympathy. I was the one who was sorry that so many people had decided to leave before I had finished.

'Oh no, that was nothing to do with you,' said the secretary. 'The last bus goes at 9.10 and those people who left early had to make sure they were on it!' I wasn't due to finish until 9.30, and nobody had thought to tell me about the last bus.

I've discovered the hard way that clairvoyants have to be prepared for all kinds of distractions. Often I am on stage battling against people slurping beer and Coca-Cola out of cans or trying hard to be heard over the rustle of crisp and sweet packets being opened and dipped into. The sudden flare of a match when a cigarette is being lit can also be very distracting. Worst of all is the small party of six or eight women sitting only a few rows back from the stage, all wanting to tell each other at the same time about the dreadful day they've had.

Try to stop them drinking, munching or chatting and they let you know in no uncertain terms that anyone on stage is just a diversion for when they've run out of conversation! Which isn't often. I've been told to 'Sod off' several times for interrupting such hen groups.

My introduction to public shows was through Derek Robinson. We are still good mates and I still bounce ideas and problems off him. He is a very experienced show presenter, so his advice is always worth hearing.

Much of my early show tuition came from Derek who worked very closely with Doris Stokes as well as the late Gordon Higginson. For me, Gordon will always be one of the most gifted British mediums.

On the other hand, Doris Stokes knew how to handle an audience but, in my opinion, she wasn't the most gifted of mediums. Her stage presence was her strength and she knew how to have an audience eating out of her hand! She also had her enemies.

One particular vicar was not on her side. In fact, the Reverend Ronald Granger was positively hostile when it leaked out that Doris and I were planning a psychic meeting in his parish at Petersfield Town Hall.

The Sun newspaper carried a whopping big headline which left Doris Stokes in no doubt that neither her physical nor spiritual presence was welcome – 'Message for Doris Stokes: get lost' it screamed.

The report went on to read: 'The angry warning was delivered by vicar Ronald Granger who claims the famous medium is "un-Christian". The Rev. Granger doesn't believe Doris really talks to the dead and he has told councillors at Petersfield in Hampshire that they should ban her from speaking in the town.'

According to this clergyman, the New Testament teaches that people don't automatically live on after death and he believed it was very unhelpful for people to believe they did.

'One has to learn to face death. I have known of many cases where people have grieved more after going to a spiritualist,' he insisted.

After this broadside from Petersfield, Doris decided to give the place a miss, adding: 'I've got no plans to visit Petersfield. Plenty of other people are only too keen to hear me.'

Maybe the vicar had a point about Doris Stokes's ability to talk to the dead. I know my view will be controversial but I have to say I always had my doubts about her psychic gift. She was a great showwoman and she exploited this skill to the full, often with a lot of meaningless waffle. She was also quickly on the blower to me, sounding off.

I was sitting at my desk in Norbury police station.

Doris was in a foul mood. 'What's this nonsense you have been telling *The Sun* about me and you being banned from Petersfield?' she snapped. It was about 8.30 a.m. and she was most irate. 'I have not been banned from anywhere,' she continued down the line. Frankly, I didn't know what she was talking about and told her so.

'Go and get a *Sun* newspaper and ring me back,' she insisted. I bought the paper, rang her back and asked her what the problem was.

'So, they got it all wrong,' I told her.

'You must have given them an interview,' she said. I told her I had not. It took about twenty minutes before she calmed down and rang off.

Her ego was easily dented as I discovered when I heard my name mentioned during a press reception that Doris had laid on on board the Orient Express. Doris had paid British Rail £100 a head for a number of reporters to be entertained on the train journey from Victoria to Hollingbourne, near Maidstone.

A reporter was talking about the Petersfield ban, so my name came into it. Doris was not amused because she thought I was using her name to gain publicity for myself.

To back off, as Doris did, when confronted by a disbeliever such as Ronald Granger, was just about the worst thing she could have done, but then, her convictions and skills as a clairvoyant were not as strong as my own.

We all owe a great deal to Doris Stokes because she did more than most in recent years to draw attention to spiritualism. In my view, clairvoyant Doris Collins will never be as popular as the late Doris Stokes. Ironically, because they shared the same Christian name, they were often confused, and this irritated Doris Collins. I was with Doris Collins on one occasion when she said she wished her name was not Doris because of the public's confusion between her and Doris Stokes.

Whatever the feeling between these two women, there is no doubt that it was Doris Stokes who, more than any other medium, in her later years, drew attention to spiritualism through her enormously successful personal appearances on stage and television and through her widely-read books. It is difficult to envisage Doris Collins ever matching this achievement and there is no way, in my opinion, that another living medium could step into Doris Stokes's shoes.

I admired Doris's ability to have an audience eating out of her hand by the sheer power of her stage charisma in emotion-charged halls, but her links with spirit were often weak.

It was my friend, Derek Robinson, who got together with Doris Stokes and Gordon Higginson, the two big guns of spiritualism, to take clairvoyance to the people through public demonstrations around Britain. Doris quickly warmed to this method of promoting spiritualism and audiences quickly warmed to her. They loved the bedside manner, the 'Hello, lovey. I have your dad with me' bit. She quickly became everybody's lovable grandmother of mediumship and they trusted her. It was a winning formula.

She appeared at the Palladium and the meeting sold out faster than an appearance by the Beatles. At Lewisham Town Hall, tickets to a Doris Stokes demonstration would go on sale at 9 a.m. but the staff went in at 6.30 a.m. to sell tea and sandwiches to the enormous queue of people who began lining up at 6 a.m. to buy tickets.

After a while she began to attract a lot of hostility, too. Newspapers began to take a long, hard look at the businesslike woman behind the lovable little-old-lady image that was Doris Stokes. There was a shrewd and powerful business machine at work and suggestions were made that, perhaps, she was not quite as honest a medium as her followers believed her to be. There was talk within spiritualist circles and the media that some people were invited by Doris Stokes to go to her meetings as her guests. A little bunch of flowers would be sent to their home, along with the invitation.

At the meeting, Doris would pick them out for a spirit message and that is why she was accused of planting recipients for her messages in her audiences. If she did, she was terribly wrong.

In her heyday, Doris Stokes was appearing before

capacity audiences up to five thousand strong. This put her under tremendous pressure to come up with good spirit links and I have no doubt that she embroidered some of these links to impress her fans. Perhaps she would have been better advised just to say, 'Sorry, ladies and gentlemen. I am not getting anything.' It happens. Then sit down, as was her style, and have a chat for ten minutes. That would have been honest but to make up messages or embellish them to impress her audience was dishonest.

Doris Stokes began in an ordinary way, then she was quite deliberately turned into a psychic superstar – for money.

Suddenly she had to perform for her huge audiences to get their money's worth. She had to come up with the goods – or flop. Superstars hate to be flops because they burn out very quickly once they fall from orbit. This pressure got to Doris and I say quite categorically that it is my belief she did cheat on occasions.

For me, Doris's credibility hit a low after I saw her in action at Wimbledon Spiritualist Church. She was on the platform in front of an audience of about three hundred people and announced that she was drawn towards a group of five women to one side of the centre aisle. Doris told them that she was linked to a young girl, a spirit child, who was walking along the aisle towards these ladies.

'Do any of you know a young girl of seven or eight

who has gone into spirit?' asked Doris. They looked blank-faced. 'She has blonde hair,' said Doris encouragingly. Still no response from the group of ladies but another woman, some six yards further on, raised her hand and said she had lost a child.

Doris picked up this lead very quickly: 'Ah, that's right, love. She has just come over to you.'

The woman added: 'Doris, I lost a son when he was nineteen.'

'That's right, love, he has just told me.'

I was left speechless and dismayed. Doris started out with a girl of eight who suddenly changed sex to become a boy of nineteen. She then passed on a message to the woman from the spirit she now said was her son. In my opinion, that was cheating.

Sorry to say this, Doris. You were an ordinary medium but an extraordinary woman. I take my hat off to you for bringing spiritualism out of the closet and for the enormous number of people who benefited from your charity. I just wish your clairvoyant honesty had not been so much in doubt.

As unimpressed as I was with Doris's psychic skills, there was no avoiding the fact that, just by watching her performances, she did teach me a lot about stage presence. In this respect she was something of a mentor and was certainly a favourite of Derek Robinson, her manager in the early days of her career and the man who was largely responsible for making her a psychic star.

Derek would tell me 'how Doris would do it', like standing, sitting or making good use of a stage. He'd say, 'Gordon Higginson stands at the microphone this way . . .' For me it was a learning process. Derek was a good teacher and I listened to him because he put on good demonstrations of clairvoyance. He couldn't afford a newcomer like me to lower his standards so I always did what he suggested.

On our way by car to meetings in various parts of Britain he'd often test me out. 'You getting anything now, Keith?' he'd ask in his strong south London accent. Sometimes I did; often I didn't.

However, I wasn't another Doris Stokes or another Gordon Higginson in my style of presentation. I was a one-off, cheeky clairvoyant who, from the very start, wanted to break all the rules of linking up with the spirit world. I have never wanted it to be a morbid, mystical, scary experience. I want it to be fun, bubbly, happy and, yes, even cheeky if the occasion calls for it. Naturally, it doesn't always.

The knack is knowing when to be humorous. Try to be funny at the wrong time and it can be disastrous. I have heard a medium on stage say, 'Your mother died of cancer, didn't she?' then giggle nervously.

If I've got someone's spirit dad with me and in life he swore like a trooper, it isn't going to convince his son sitting out there in my audience if I tell him his dad is a very serious man. 'That's not my dad,' he'd be quick to tell me.

So if I can say, 'He isn't half going on a bit, swearing, laughing, joking. If only you could hear what your dad is saying to me . . .' then he knows I've got his dad! It also gets the audience going. They love it.

At first, some audiences may think I am being a bit rude or disrespectful at the expense of either the spirit person I have with me or the audience contact.

At one meeting I located a young girl named Clare in my audience, after I'd made contact with her dead father. At first, I could see I wasn't convincing Clare that I really did have her spirit father with me so I asked him to tell me something positive about his daughter. He responded by telling me that Clare had a white teddy bear on her bed which her mum had bought for her twenty-first birthday.

However, instead of passing on the message in this routine sort of way, I said to Clare: 'Can I come to your bedroom with you? Is that OK, Clare?'

She became very shy and was not quite sure what to say because she hadn't a clue what I was getting at. People started laughing. I carried on ribbing her, 'Come on Clare, I only want to take you to your bedroom for a minute . . .'

Then I explained to her how her dad was telling me about the teddy bear her mum gave her for her twenty-first. I know it might be considered a bit cheeky to tease girls like Clare but it made the message that much more interesting and it was great for holding everyone's attention.

It is especially satisfying for me when I can bring comfort to someone who has lost a loved one to spirit, as in the case of a lady named Sylvia Hillier.

I am indebted to reporter Natalie Gray for the following account:

'A mother says she has had beyond-the-grave talks with her dead son who drowned in a river tragedy three years ago.

'Sylvia Hillier says her son has even described to her how he died, thus offering a clue to the mystery of the death crash which baffled police and other experts.

'Graham, her youngest son, drowned with his friend, Anthony Cater, when their car plunged into the Thames at Shepperton. No one, until now, had been able to explain how the car ended up in the river.

'Though rumours were rife, no one reported seeing or hearing anything on that fateful night.

'Mrs Hillier, of Greenwood Close, Woodham, is now convinced she has solved the mystery, thanks to Keith Charles – a policeman and medium – who recently claimed to have also been in touch with tragic toddler Ben Hardwick.

'Mr Charles, from Chessington, visited Mrs Hillier's home and gave her what she believes is a vivid account of how her younger son died.

' "I didn't know him from Adam," explained Mrs Hillier, 50, "yet he came into my room and told me so much about the accident it was almost as if he had been there."

'Mr Charles described a security van going the wrong way up the one-way tow path with its headlights full on. He even managed to recall half the registration number.

' "I believe Graham and Anthony swerved to avoid the oncoming van and, because the road is so narrow, they ended up in the river," said Mrs Hillier. "There must have been some sort of an impact with the van, because the car had a smashed wing when it was hauled out of the river."

'Mrs Hillier said she had quizzed her son, through Mr Charles, about whether he had been drinking that night. She was told that all he had was a lager with a lemonade top. A post-mortem confirmed that Graham had drunk only a small quantity of alcohol.

'Mrs Hillier said her son told her he was OK, and predicted that his elder brother, Nigel, would go out with, and eventually marry, his best friend's girlfriend. Coincidence or not, that is exactly what happened . . .'

I never did actually work with Doris Stokes on the platform, but I did work with Gordon Higginson.

One such occasion was at Birmingham Town Hall when the other guest clairvoyant, Doris Collins, couldn't make it and I stepped in. Another time with Gordon was at Glasgow Town Hall on 26 September 1984. Gordon Higginson was a tremendous man who was president of the Spiritualist National Union right up to his death. He was a medium for some fifty years.

That Glasgow meeting was the first big one for me. There must have been nearly two thousand people in the audience. Apart from the fact that the date is clearly marked in my old diary, I remember it for another, funny reason.

Derek has a son named Ray who is also a very talented medium, and Ray has a 'spirit helper' named Thomas. Derek wanted to know if I was going to be all right on my first big night so Ray was able to tell his dad that if he asked me for a name, I would reply 'Thomas'. His guide, Thomas, would watch over me and make sure I came up with the goods.

On the way up to Glasgow in the train Derek kept asking me to give him a name, the first name that came into my head. 'Oh, I don't know, how about Mary?' I suggested.

'No, no, no. Not Mary. Try again,' said Derek.

'Jack?' No, no, no. 'What about Tony?'

'No, no, no,' said Derek impatiently. He kept up this game for quite a while until he decided it was time for what we called a little Jack and Dandy. This is Derek's pet name for brandy! Oh, why not. So Derek hopped off and soon returned with cups of coffee and the brandies. 'Give us another name, Keith.'

'Fred?'

'No, not Fred.'

We reached Glasgow and booked into our hotel. After a quick wash, we went straight down to the town hall to check out how many tickets had been sold – over a thousand and they were still selling. Great! 'Give us a name, Keith,' snapped Derek, still hoping I was going to come up with Thomas, but, yet again, I didn't.

By now Derek was desperate and beginning to think my evening was going to go down the plug hole.

In any case, I was getting browned off with his silly game, being asked to come up with a name off the top of my head every five minutes.

The huge audience was now seated. We took our places on the platform alongside Gordon Higginson and the meeting opened. As the host welcomed us all, Gordon leaned across to me and whispered, 'You should be forming your link now, Keith.'

'Thanks, Gordon.' It was quite an occasion for me, not far off being a rookie, to be on the platform with one of Britain's best-ever mediums and standing in for Doris Collins. With some two thousand Doris Collins fans disappointed that their Doris was not able to be there, it certainly wasn't the time for me to blow it.

Then came my introduction: 'Ladies and gentleman – Keith Charles, one of our new and very talented younger mediums.'

I was on for the next twenty minutes. I caught Derek looking hard at me from the side of the stage, still challenging me to give him the right name. Then an extraordinary thing happened. As I stood up, everyone seemed to turn into gold statues. It was weird. Nothing like this had ever happened to me before. I thought I was going to pass out. I looked again ... everyone seemed to have a gold aura wrapped round them.

What could it be? Was it my nervousness, was it spirit or something else? The gold aura images must have lasted only a split second or so but it seemed an eternity to me. I called on spirit to give me some help. I needed a lead. 'Is there a lady here named Mrs Stewart?' I called out.

Then my apparent stupidity hit me. We were in Scotland, it would have been a miracle if there hadn't been a Mrs Stewart in the audience! The hall was probably packed with Stewarts. 'I don't care how many Stewarts there are here, please raise your hands,' I asked them. I was drawn to one side of the huge hall, to one particular lady, and, as it happened, the only Mrs Stewart present. I told her I had her husband with me who was saying that his name was – Thomas!

'That was his name,' said Mrs Stewart.

From then on I just flowed with spirit contacts and messages. I was given a very warm reception. Afterwards, Derek was amazed that I had come up with the name 'Thomas' with my very first contact. He said he'd been asking me all day for the name Thomas and I hadn't given it. We both thanked spirit.

When I began going on stage, Derek used to press a little cross into my hand. I'd slip it into my pocket. It's Derek's cross but I still use it. I see it as a form of protection, a thank you to God. Maybe that cross had worked its wonders for me at that first meeting.

I have to say that I often do feel very close to God when I am on stage. I even feel holy. When I have finished, though, I just can't stop talking – and I can always murder a drink. Clairvoyance is very thirsty work.

I'm not much of a drinker but after the successful Glasgow meeting Derek and I were invited back to the home of a young man named Gordon Kennedy, Scotland's Musician of the Year. With Gordon and his mum and dad we had a few drinks and a bit of a sing-song, then it was back to our hotel where Derek and I shared a room – in single beds, of course!

We thought we'd have a nightcap, so we asked our porter, Ronnie, to bring a couple of brandies to our room, which he did. Then we fancied peanuts, so Ronnie had to go back downstairs to the bar and get our peanuts. By the time he returned to our room with the peanuts, we had finished our drinks and decided it would be a good idea to have another. Off went Ronnie for more drinks. We were paying him a generous tip each time so he didn't seem to mind the service we asked of him.

We lined up our bottles on a wooden shelf which ran round our room. Derek had the poor guy running up and down stairs all night, so in the end we nicknamed him 'Run, Ronnie, Run'.

Ronnie woke us the next morning at 6.30 with a beer each 'on the house', thinking it would give us plenty of time to have breakfast and allow time for us to be on our train which left at 9.30 a.m.

Unfortunately, we sank our beers and went off to sleep again until 11 a.m. We missed our breakfast and our train and had to settle for breakfast at a nearby cafe and a much later train back to London.

These particular stories don't have a great deal to do with being a policeman or a psychic but I tell them to show what life can be like for this particular touring clairvoyant! Because I know I have a spirit life to look forward to, I fully enjoy my earthly life as well. Unfortunately, this cannot be said of a good many clairvoyants who seem to take themselves, and spiritualism, much too seriously. It is as if they believe they must present a public image of total sobriety and dowdiness. As though for someone to believe in the afterlife, he or she must be boring too. What nonsense! This is certainly not the way Derek Robinson and I see it, as you will have gathered.

Even so, there is a time to be serious, and respectful.

At a meeting in Hove, the spirit of a boy of sixteen, killed while riding pillion on a motorcyle, communicated through me to a man in the audience but how could this man believe I was really linked to the spirit of his friend? The spirit boy gave me the precise time he died – 11.35. It was spot on and, to press home the evidence of the spirit boy's survival beyond this life, he 'showed' me his distinctive leather wallet, which I then described. The young man in the audience recognised it immediately as the one his friend had on him when he was killed.

When so-called psychic sleuth, American James Randi, told us Britons in his television series that there is no such thing as life after death, the British public was quick to tell him he had got it all wrong!

It was the *Daily Star* which put together some of its readers' amazing stories.

Margaret Noble wrote in to say that she no longer doubts that it is possible for the dead to make contact with the living. She was holding a china dog, much loved by her dead mother, and the room was silent except for the ticking of a clock on the mantelpiece. At precisely 3 p.m., the clock stopped. 'When my mother died, I visited her house. At exactly 3 p.m. a musical box started to play, which I believe was her way of telling me not to worry.'

Margaret believes that when she was holding the china dog and the clock again stopped at 3 p.m.

precisely, it was again her mother, reassuring her that she is still around in spirit.

The time of 3 p.m. was also the spiritual message received by Sara Brinn when she was a child. She ran to her mother and announced her dad had died at 3 p.m.

'I got spanked for being cruel,' said Mrs Brinn, of Gorton near Manchester. 'But later we received a telegram saying my father had died at 3 p.m. – the time I'd told my mum.'

I was on live radio and disc jockey Johnnie Walker asked me: 'Do you try and convince people there is life after death?'

I told Johnnie and his radio audience that nobody has to be a believer to go along to a demonstration. I explained that my purpose is to try to take the sting out of death. Clairvoyants like me know we can never replace the physical presence of someone who has passed into spirit, but the love for family and friends will always come through. Unfortunately, however, we are not like disc jockeys and cannot do requests! We don't call up spirits; they call on us and when they do it is reassurance they want to give to those they have loved and left behind. That is why it is seemingly trivial messages that they will pass on, not big issues.

It is important to those in spirit that we know they are happy and that they know those they have left behind are not still grieving. They understand the need to prove beyond doubt their existence in spirit, which means imparting some kind of 'identification' through the clairvoyant.

The only way to be convinced, if you are not convinced already, is to pop along to a psychic meeting and see for yourself.

CHAPTER EIGHT

LIFE AFTER DEATH

God is the creator of everything, absolutely everything. He is the boss. However, suggest this to scientists and most of them will be quick to disagree as though they know all the answers. They do not.

Ask scientists to create a seed that will become a plant. They can't do it. So they haven't got all the answers to life – or, for that matter, to death.

Scientists, like many ordinary people, measure their beliefs along the lines of what they will accept is

127

precisely what they can see. If they cannot see it, touch it, prove it, then their attitude is that it cannot be possible!

Some people are like that with spiritualism. Until they get a message, until it is proved to them, they will not believe contact with spirit is possible. I am not saying this attitude is necessarily wrong but when a person comes to one of my demonstrations, at least that person is opening up his or her mind to contact with spirit being possible.

I am inviting these people to look, and try to see, what I know does exist. If they will not even allow themselves to take a look, how can they possibly become aware?

That is all I ask of anyone: that they allow themselves to take a look. There is no need for me to cram my awareness of life after death down their throats because I know people will quickly see it for themselves if they just give themselves the chance.

People such as James Randi, the American psychic investigator, and Britain's international magician, Paul Daniels, claim that they can perform anything a medium can do. All I would say is that magicians are very much in control of their own ability to create illusions or perform trickery. They manipulate. However, as a medium on stage giving a demo, I cannot manipulate and I am certainly not in control of the situation, other than that I pass on messages I receive from spirit.

The only test of my ability is if the recipient, from his or her own knowledge of the spirit, can relate to the information I pass on. If they cannot, then I am either a clever rogue or I have my lines crossed! I know I am not the former but, occasionally, I might initially pass on messages to the wrong person. Then it is up to me to make sure I find the correct recipient by careful questioning.

So, why should anyone believe there is a God?

Many of us don't get to meet the Queen, or even to see her in the flesh, but we know she exists and we know she is within our reach if we go through the right channels. It's the same with God. I know he exists but I haven't met him, although I know I will eventually – perhaps not on my next level of spiritual development, or even the one after that, but eventually.

Will I recognise him when I see him? Is God black, white, yellow? Is God a man, or even a woman? Is he fat, is he thin? Does he wear a gown, or jacket and trousers?

If you gave a classroom of kids in Britain, Africa and China a sketchpad and asked them to draw a picture of God, I know you would have three entirely different kinds of pictures. However, what the kids would all be saying is that they believe in the existence of God, regardless of what he looks like.

If I asked you, the reader, to describe yourself without looking in a mirror, it is quite probable that your description would not look anything like your true physical shape.

It is the same when we go to the spirit world. The power of our spirit allows us to imagine our shape to be whatever we want it to be.

The film *Ghost* showed brilliantly the physical and spiritual body separating at death.

Terrible things happen to physical bodies. They get mutilated, drowned, beheaded or can die of heartache. It is quite shocking! Bodies can be eaten alive by disease before dying. What we do know is that, in the end, the body is discarded, rather like an overcoat, after it has served its purpose in earthly life, allowing the spirit to cross into the spirit world which is all about us.

I try to explain this 'changeover' by describing how spirit goes to a recovery room, a kind of spirit world hospital. Imagine the anguish of your spirit on its lonely travels in a completely new environment immediately after death. The spirit world takes care of this by ensuring you are met by someone you knew on Earth. Suddenly the shock of death turns into the happiness and reassurance of meeting a friend or a departed loved one.

The spirit recovery area is where we come to terms with death and our new life in spirit. I will probably meet my dear old grandad to whom I was especially close when he was alive. If I was to die now, he would probably be there to welcome me.

That reunion might go something like this: 'Hello, Keith. You have died and I am here to welcome you into your new life.'

'How did I die, Grandad?' I might well ask him because so often we either don't know we have actually died or we haven't a clue how it happened, especially if it was traumatic.

Grandad would show me how I died if I needed to know so that I'd understand and accept my fate.

If, in your physical life, you do not believe in life after death, you would not expect to find yourself in the spirit world.

You can consciously tell yourself there is no life after death because that is your conscious body speaking. Your spiritual being – that inner energy which is the real you – is well aware of there being life after death.

So my grandad would make it quite clear to me that I had died and that I was now in the spirit world. I would then ask, 'Grandad, where are all the people I knew when I was over on the other side?'

We would meet up but families and friends in the spirit world do not stay together any more than they do in the material world. This idea saddens some people who like to think they will become united for ever with everyone they lost in the material world. However, any such meeting lasts only for the time it is necessary.

When I go to work in this life, I don't take my wife

and kids with me. I don't take my mum and dad with me, nor my aunt and uncle. We all lead separate lives, and we are all learning separate lessons.

This is the reason for our spirit spending time in the 'recovery area'. It is here that we renew old acquaintances. When we know they are fine and they know we are fine, everyone moves on. We are beginning to understand our spiritual consciousness and are coming to terms with life in this new world.

As a baby needs to be taught how to feed itself, how to walk and how to talk in order to fulfil its material needs, so our spirit needs to be taught how to function in the spirit world.

Sometimes I can pick up the strong spirit of someone who has recently passed over. That spirit still has strong earthly pulls; their will is desperate to reassure those they have left behind that they are in good spirits, so to speak! In such a situation, I might say to my dead grandad, 'I just want to pop back and tell Chris [my second wife] that I am all right. I want my kids to know I am all right.' If my will is strong enough then I will do this.

On Earth, if your will and your belief are strong enough concerning life after death, you will want to contact your loved ones who have passed into spirit. They will be equally reassured that you have understood what has happened and that you are not grieving for them.

When I was at police training school, another cadet

told me how he had woken in the early hours of one morning when his fiancee was due to fly back from a holiday in Spain. He couldn't sleep. A bit later that morning, over breakfast, his postman father made a cup of tea and handed it to his son who suddenly dropped the cup which smashed on the floor. 'Oh, my God, Mary is dead!' he shouted in anguish to his father.

His father said, 'What do you mean, Mary is dead? She can't be, she doesn't even fly until nine.' They later learned that Mary had taken an earlier plane and it had crashed, killing everyone on board.

At the moment my policeman pal dropped his cup of tea, he was 'touched' by the spirit of Mary, his fiancee, who had just died in the plane crash.

The thing to try to accept is that this is spirit saying 'goodbye', trying to reassure a loved one that their spirit lives on, only in another dimension. It is perfectly natural; many people will have had this moving experience when a loved one has suddenly passed to the other side.

I suppose it is natural for people to want to know what it is like in the spirit world. I am often asked, and all I can really do is give them an idea based on accounts given by spirit to me and to other clairvoyant colleagues.

As a child, I believed that Heaven was above and beyond the clouds. I thought that people who had died actually walked around on clouds, and then moved into a world above these clouds which I believed to be Heaven. That's how I saw it as a kid of seven but, of course, once you have been in an aeroplane, that illusion is quickly shattered.

Ask fifty spiritualists to describe Heaven and I know they would all say different things. It is hardly surprising. They haven't been there, so how can they possibly describe it?

Some, more spiritually developed, mediums have visions. My own visions of life in the spirit world reveal no houses and no cars, so no traffic problems. But there is spiritual traffic, which means people like us walking about.

When we get to the spirit world, we don't know what spirit looks like. If I said to you, as from two o'clock today we will be in Heaven, how could you possibly know what to expect? How would we know what to expect to look like at one minute past two? Equally, we wouldn't know what was expected of us. I believe we shall be what we want to be and shall take on the shape most familiar to us, with a few amendments. If I want to be a bit slimmer, I shall be a bit slimmer. Those who may want to be a bit younger can be a bit younger.

So you are what you want to be. It is not a transparent shape, more a transparency of ourselves, and yet it is not a physical shape as we know it on Earth. We take on an intangible shape, which is why people say they see ghosts. The energy that spirit creates to come back and make itself visible is only a form which spirit knows will be recognisable to those who are alive.

Perhaps an easier way to understand how spirits probably 'see' themselves, and others, is to think of someone you know well and conjure up his or her image in your mind's eye. That image would represent another spirit.

So, for the first period in the spirit world we are this transparency. We do exist there in a kind of spiritual solidity, but not a physical one.

Remember, we left the physical part of our being behind, meaning our body. If the manner in which we left this world hasn't totally ruined our body (perhaps by being burned, mutilated or whatever) then those we leave behind make sure the body is of no further use to us or anyone else (other than for some spare parts used in transplants) by burning or burying it. This doesn't matter. Our spirit, the real energy which is us, has long gone.

It is a pity that more people don't think this way. If the body we leave behind at death is empty because spirit has vacated it, then why not put the bits to good use? Let the man next door, who is going blind, have my eyes; have a surgeon take out my heart and give it to the lady over the road. These organs are no longer any use to me once I have departed to the spirit world.

We do this with cars, so think of death as a kind

of breaker's yard. If a car is no good, it may well end up in a breaker's yard, where somebody else can make use of a bonnet, a door panel or whatever. We know that car is effectively dead, that it won't ever be good enough to be driven again, but it still has its uses.

Spirit is the life force and our bodies cannot function without it. A scientist will say that a body cannot function without a heart so, when that packs up, the body dies. When physical life is no longer sustainable, the spirit moves on.

The first stage of spirit life is like a holiday, but a holiday that is not measured by time. There is no 'time' in the spirit world – no clocks, no watches. Time is man-made, not something dreamed up by God.

We arrive in Heaven with memories of the physical world but without any physical disabilities. So, if I was legless when I was alive, I could have my legs back in the next world because there are no such things as legs in spirit; they become a part of our spirit transparency.

Interestingly, this is why psychic artists like Coral Polge will often draw a picture of a spirit person showing themselves to Coral at an age in their mortal life when they liked themselves best.

I have heard it said that there are halls of learning over there. Does this mean centres like universities? Probably not, but 'learning centres', where lesser-developed spirits can be helped to progress are definitely a part of spirit life.

Perhaps the question I am asked most of all by people is: 'When I die will I meet up with the child I lost?'

The answer is 'yes'. Families meet up whether you have had three husbands or six wives. It doesn't matter, you all meet again in the spirit world but there is no worldly animosity, no bitterness, no pain, just joy. You meet, feel at ease in your new environment and move on.

If I had murdered my wife on Earth, and later died, we would meet up in spirit but there would be no bitterness, no hate, no jealousy. These are all human emotions which we leave behind. Only the all-embracing feeling of love exists in spirit. This is where the so-called halls of learning or learning centres, as I prefer to call them, come into their own. Murderers are taught that the taking of life is not tolerated.

In spirit, this learning is going on all the time. Spirit must be taught, just like humans. That is why I say to people, with half a smile, that they don't die and suddenly sprout wings and become angels overnight! Just because they are dead, it does not give them a passport to holiness. We take our experiences, our earthly misdeeds, with us which is why there is a need in the spirit world for learning centres.

I am asked if people take disease with them, such as cancer. No they do not.

What about reincarnation? Do people die, go into spirit, then return to human life again? From the teachings I have received from my spiritual guides, there is reincarnation for some.

Reincarnation is the return of a spiritual life from Heaven back into an earthly life. It happens to those who have missed out on particular lessons in this life. It is, perhaps, a bit like being downgraded at school. A pupil needs to go back to a lower class to go over, and pick up on, lessons they haven't yet absorbed.

I do not believe that life on Earth is the inception of spirit. Earth is not Class One. We are spirit before we come to Earth. So, unless we are a reincarnated spirit, we are new to this Earth. I don't want mothers panicking, thinking that their babies are reincarnated spirits; it is possible but unlikely.

There is also a good chance that, on Earth, we sometimes 'carry' student spirits needing to learn lessons that we on Earth may be learning. The spirit attaches itself to us and shadows us, although, of course, we would have no idea this was happening.

Let's take stress. Supposing, on Earth, I am going through a particularly stressful time and a spirit, whom I will call 'Mr X', happens to need to learn how to cope with the same kind of stress which caused him to take his own earthly life by suicide. So, Mr X walks with me – and learns. He may be with me for a day, a month, a year; the length of time doesn't matter. Only a psychic might sense that this was happening. Mr X then moves on in his spiritual development, having learned how he should have coped better with physical stress.

I am not saying that these views are necessarily ones held by all spiritualists or clairvoyants but they are responses from spirit to questions put to me. I then ask spirit guides for the answers.

Heaven is all around us and is not a separate place up in the sky or on Planet X. The spirit world is in a different dimension but is still where we are. That is why I can stand up at one of my meetings and say to someone in my audience: 'This morning at eight you put on a pair of brown shoes but suddenly changed your mind and wore black shoes instead. I know that because your dad, in spirit, is telling me he saw you.' That spirit dad has got to be in this world to see it happen.

Everybody understands what a television is but to work that television it is necessary to push the 'on' button. Once that is pushed, we can see what is being transmitted.

Right, so my grandad has been dead for twenty-four years. If he wants to see how I am getting on, he has to push his 'on' button to look into my world. If he feels he needs to influence me in some way, then he will do so. Call it psychic, call it instinct, but most of us have experienced this kind of help at one time or another. It is probably from spirit.

Sometimes my views on life after death are controversial but this doesn't necessarily make them wrong. Besides, I put my trust in my spirit guides and what they tell me.

There was one occasion when this wasn't good enough for a certain lady at one of my meetings at the City Hall in Sheffield. This woman wanted to know what happened to babies when they go to the spirit world. When I told her that they grow up and develop spiritually, this woman asked me, 'So you disagree with Doris Stokes?'

I had to tell her that I had no idea of Doris Stokes's views on the matter, so this woman explained that Doris had said in one of her books that children who die are kept in capsules waiting for their mums to go to the spirit world.

I had to tell the lady that if this was Doris Stokes's explanation, I totally disagreed. Then came the cruncher. The woman told me: 'Well, you're wrong because Doris Stokes said so!' That is how people can create an image of somebody like Doris Stokes and believe that they can say no wrong. I do not claim that everything I say, or write here, is necessarily one hundred per cent correct, but I do *believe* it to be correct.

The idea that a baby dies and is put in a capsule until its mother joins it in spirit, maybe sixty years later, is totally unacceptable to me. It would also be totally selfish. I do not believe spirit works this way, so I still maintain that Doris Stokes was wrong to say that it does.

Clairvoyants, spiritualists and mediums do not always agree. There is so much speculation about the form of life after death that there is bound to be disagreement. There is even disagreement involving the two representative bodies relating to spiritualism, the Spiritualists' National Union and the Christian Spiritualists.

In principle, the Christian Spiritualists accept the leadership of Jesus Christ, whereas the Spiritualists' National Union does not. This is a bit like the differences between Catholicism and the Church of England – different views under the same religious banner.

The SNU does not believe that Jesus was the son of God, nor do I. I believe we are all the sons and daughters of God. To me, Jesus was a highly evolved spirit, a special spirit who came to Earth at a time when He was most needed. If He was around now He would be a superstar, more powerful than Billy Graham; even more powerful than the Pope.

Jesus stood on a mountain and spoke to many thousands without a PA system; He created miracles of healing, which we do in churches today.

Billy Graham doesn't heal people. The Pope is a very powerful man, as are other religious leaders, but none of them does what Jesus was reported to have done as revealed in the Bible. Jesus was a very special spirit.

I suppose a parallel might be Neil Armstrong walking on the Moon. How many people even believed we could fire a rocket to the Moon, manoeuvre it to land on the surface and then witness the astronauts getting out and walking about?

But how much about Jesus was true? Probably no more than eight per cent. The kind of miracles Jesus performed now happen every day and yet I have no doubts that He was a very highly evolved spirit who came to Earth to bring people together.

I believe that Winston Churchill, who has communicated with us since his earthly death, did much the same thing but we never called him the Son of God, although he saved Britain and Europe from the tyranny of Hitler. If Churchill had been given the same credence as Jesus, I see no reason why he should not have been upheld as another Messiah. I am not trying to compare Churchill with Jesus, but to emphasise the image which humans create, to show how powerful this can be to those under this influence.

We do not put many humans closer to God, in our earthly esteem, than the Pope, and yet nobody calls him the Son of God or claims that his spirit has descended from Heaven to save us all. Our intelligence and awareness are now so much more than they were two thousand years ago. We know better. Fewer people now accept religion parrot-fashion. They want a lot more from religion than just to stand up in church and hear the twenty-third psalm read as it has been read this year, last year and every year. That is why they are now looking more to spiritualism with some of their questions about life and death, which have remained unanswered for so long.

People are inquisitive, prepared to question their own faith and the faiths of others in a relentless search to find the truth. Those who fear this search will throw up red herrings, such as the danger of ouija boards, in an effort to discredit spiritualism. In fact, ouija boards have no place in spiritualism.

A number of my showbusiness clients think very deeply about life after death, perhaps because, as finely tuned artists, they are that much closer to the soul than, say, a more earthly, physical person such as a manual worker. They often have interesting views on what it will be like in Heaven.

CHAPTER NINE

GIVING SPIRITS A BAD NAME

Ask most people what image they have of spiritualism and they will probably tell you it is of a group of little old ladies sitting around a table in a darkened room, touching fingers spread out over a dark oak table, with a Madame Arcati figure leading a seance and calling out in a droning, emotionless voice: 'Is there anyone there wanting to talk to us?'

Summoning up the spirit world in this manner has been most people's idea of spritualism since it became the object of increased public curiosity in the late 1940s, largely through cinema images of Madame Arcati in the film *Blithe Spirit*, played by that wonderful, bumbling character actress, Margaret Rutherford.

When she went into a trance and brought 'the other world' into her living room, all kinds of weird and wonderful things happened, most of them hilarious, most portrayed as trickery, all under the label of entertainment. So it was not surprising that few people at the time took those little old ladies, Madame Arcati and spiritualism too seriously.

Unfortunately, this image and reputation still linger on but, in my opinion, this is because spiritualist followers mostly insist on hiding themselves away, ostrich-fashion, in the obscurity and ignorance of those earlier days.

Spiritualism needs a good prod to bring it swiftly into the twenty-first century and it is my intention, as one of spiritualism's younger – and probably more outspoken – followers, to play my part in spreading a greater understanding about the truth and effectiveness of mediumship.

The Madame Arcatis are still around and you can spot their tiny advertisements in the personal columns of many local newspapers, but they are a diminishing breed, more and more pigeon-holed for their entertainment value rather than for their psychic gift. Many of them have side-stepped a bit in an attempt to be fashionable and to create a demand for their services by describing what they do as astrology.

If they really want to lay on the syrup, then they call themselves psychic astrologers! Most of them have about as much developed psychic intuition as Madame Arcati, and far less entertainment value. I really don't mean to be unkind but I wish many fringe psychics would stop giving spiritualism and genuine, practising mediums a bad name. It is bad enough that spiritualism cannot seem to cast off its boring, dowdy, old-fashioned reputation, without having every Tom, Dick and Harriet tarnishing its image still further.

Old women who sit on piers reading tea leaves, Tarot cards and palms are seldom genuinely gifted mediums, whatever they might advertise as or seek to tell their clients. They have developed a nice line in patter which gives the punter a ray of hope, usually about love, money and work. It is seldom worth the £10–30 that they charge.

If spiritualism could clean up and modernise its act, this would go a long way to removing the stigma which still drags it down. Even the media tend to look upon us as freaks who have crawled out of the woodwork. They come to us around Hallowe'en and beg us to go on television to take part in some chat show, only to spend the interview questioning our sincerity and ability.

In Britain, radio and television personality Terry Wogan is an old hand at this! American so-called psychic investigator James Randi (a former magician) challenged the good reputations of several British mediums with equal efficiency.

Both achieved this on television shows hosted by themselves and over which they had effective control. Victims included British mediums Stephen O'Brien, Coral Polge, Carmen Rogers and Marion Martinez.

When self-proclaimed American psychic investigator James Randi stormed into Britain with his own television series, he did his best to knock the stuffing out of the idea of life after death.

In a press release issued by Granada TV, Randi pronounced:

'In order to accept things like mediumship and spiritualism you have to accept separation of body and mind, or, if you want, soul.

'Since there is no evidence whatsoever for soul and it is entirely a matter of faith, I have no conviction in the matter.

'Survival after death has never been established, despite the fact that the Society for Psychical Research is now more than a century old. They admit they have never come up with one positive experiment.

'But they are always announcing they are on the verge of an imminent breakthrough. They said the same thing on their inauguration in the 1870s.

'Spiritualism is a big thing in Britain, which is

interesting when you consider it is an American invention and it is now almost unheard of over there, except in California and Florida. Californians believe in everything and the average age of people in Florida is deceased. It is known as God's waiting room, so it is in their interests to believe.'

So much for James Randi's pronouncements. He clearly doesn't believe in life after death for the human spirit or the human soul.

I learned that Randi was offering ten thousand dollars to anyone who could prove there was life after death, an offer, he says, which had remained unclaimed for twenty-five years. I agreed to take up that challenge through the *News of the World*. The paper contacted Randi in America.

At his home in Fort Lauderdale, the American conjuror said he was very pleased the British medium Keith Charles wanted his money – but the challenge couldn't go ahead because of the unreasonable conditions he placed on it.

Randi told the Sunday newspaper that his conditions for accepting the challenge were that the psychic cop 'talked' to a dead man whose background had been researched and was known in detail to Mr Randi. I had to tell him that this was just not on. I told the *News of the World*, 'Does Mr Randi think we mediums have a person-to-person telephone line to everyone in the spirit world? That all we have to do is dial through? Of course we don't.' The condition was unreasonable and impractical.

I put my own conditions forward. Let Mr Randi choose any one, or more, of my twenty psychic meetings held in towns and cities throughout Britain. He could come and hear for himself how I communicate with the dead and the kind of information which they give to identify themselves to their earthly loved ones. For the people who come to my meetings, and who are contacted, there is no doubt. Let a panel of independent judges decide and let Mr Randi investigate the people who are randomly communicated with, to ensure I haven't 'planted' them in my audience.

My only other condition was that Mr Randi's money be held by an independent party so that he could not change his mind when the decision went against him!

The *News of the World* drew a blank. James Randi didn't want to know any more – and my challenge was never taken up.

Randi's show, the first of a series on the paranormal made by Granada Television, which went out nationally on 17 July 1991, suggested to some ten million viewers that what these 'psychic guinea pigs' did was misguided and misleading because they failed Randi's entertaining tests.

How many times have I had people say to me, 'Can

you prove it is possible to contact the dead?'

I always answer, 'Can you prove I cannot?' I have had many experiences and much evidence to satisfy me that there is a spirit link between this world and the next. However, when there is a trial by television of a medium's ability to speak to spirit, it is largely for entertainment value, so the tests are seldom fair.

So often mediums are to blame for their own downfall. They agree to take part in television shows because the invitation is flattering, so it is no good them complaining when they are hung, drawn and quartered in front of millions of viewers!

Talented psychic artist Coral Polge doesn't need the likes of James Randi to tell the world about her undoubted gifts but when she was invited to allow this gift to be tested on one of his television shows, she accepted. She asked me if I considered it a good idea and I told her I thought she would be unwise to accept, unless she had the guarantee of a fair hearing.

She didn't lay down specific conditions to guarantee fairness, so the resulting appearance was a disaster. She was made to look silly. She did no favours to herself nor to spiritualism and she ended up regretting the whole affair.

Terry Wogan doesn't appear to like spiritualists either. Each time I have seen him interviewing mediums, the audience ends up laughing at them.

Carmen Rogers and Marion Martinez will never forget their encounter with this man for a Hallowe'en night television programme. There, again, perhaps the two women had only themselves to blame for taking part in a show about witches. Clairvoyance has nothing whatsoever to do with witches. How naïve can people be?

After he had virtually crucified Carmen and Marion on air, the interview over, Wogan said to the studio audience: 'What did you think of that? Wasn't it a load of old rubbish?' Yet by this time the mediums were not even there to defend themselves. It is this kind of remark which seems to spiritualists to be so unfair, yet, sadly, so predictable.

Stephen O'Brien is, in fact, a competent medium, but those who saw him on Wogan's show would not have thought so. Stephen was given twenty minutes on air to demonstrate his psychic ability, a rather more generous time allowance than most mediums receive. Unfortunately, Stephen homed in on one particular woman in the audience whom he believed was the correct recipient of his spirit messages, when she clearly was not. To every question Stephen put to her, she answered 'No'. So Stephen spent twenty minutes in front of nearly fifteen million viewers making a fool of himself!

A couple of days later, after Stephen's poor performance had been splashed across the national newspapers, he suddenly announced that he should have addressed his messages to a lady behind the one who could only say 'No'. Apparently, the correct recipient had sent him a letter to let him know that she had understood everything he had said, that it all applied to her!

Poor Stephen came off the air with his tail between his legs, suffering from an overdose of humiliation.

'You didn't do very well, did you Stephen?' chided Wogan. Stephen acknowledged his poor performance, which probably put back the cause of spiritualism a good ten years.

So, how should he have handled the situation? For a start, I would like to see clairvoyants who flatter themselves that they should be seen on television, learn how to cope with the complexities of television. Wogan had to. He didn't just suddenly host one of television's most popular peak-viewing shows without knowing what he was doing.

Yet, mediums think they can enter this alien world of bright lights, cameras and audiences so controlled that they are even told when to clap, and expect to get away without a scratch. Of course, they can't. Used in the right way, television can put over the right message more powerfully than any other area of mass communication. Put over badly, it can be totally destructive. Who, in their right mind, would attempt to defuse an unexploded bomb unless they had been fully trained to do so? Mediums need to be taught how to behave, how to act, how to react in a situation like this.

I have had that training, along with the experience

of several television appearances and still more live radio interviews and phone-ins. It is necessary to build up confidence and to know what you have let yourself in for *before* you set out along this route. The fact that mediums perform their clairvoyance on stage, in front of an audience, means that we have a bit of showbusiness in us. We must like the attention but we misuse it at our peril.

The fact is that giving out spirit messages on a time-restricted television show does not make good television.

A medium cannot rush his or her contact with those in the spirit world and they seldom react in a way that suits the medium. You can say, 'Come on, spirit, show us a bit of consideration. Terry Wogan won't wait all day!' Somehow I don't think the spirit world is too concerned!

It can be even more self-defeating when a clairvoyant's performance is edited into a television programme slot. The need to condense creates distortion, sometimes accidental, more often intentional.

Anyone who saw how the guests of James Randi were edited into his show will know what I mean. They weren't given a real opportunity to perform at their best. For the same reason, I wouldn't demonstrate clairvoyance in a television studio but I would agree to a film unit coming to one of my meetings. Then we could sit down afterwards and discuss the content. 'You want to show a bad spirit message? All right, but make sure you show a good one, too,' is the way I'd want it handled. All I would expect was the right balance.

I am happy to talk about my clairvoyance on television and have done so on a number of occasions. I would also give colour readings to a television audience, as I have done many times on radio. Despite this, I am comfortable on television because I am in control of what I do. If I feel this control is slipping away from me, for whatever reason, then I very quickly bring my performance back on line – or stop.

So, if Mr Wogan, or someone in the studio audience, gives me a hard time, as happened to Stephen O'Brien, then I would take back control and seek out the recipient for my spirit message with more conviction, or just stop.

I know that a lot of people, including spiritualists, complained about the way Stephen O'Brien came over on *Wogan*, and yet, within a week, his theatre appearances were a sellout. Perhaps he didn't do such a bad job, after all! As I say, he does speak well about life after death and he is a fine medium. Everyone is entitled to at least one mistake. Let's hope that memorable one with Wogan was Stephen's!

Personally, I like radio phone-in programmes and I have done many around Britain, including Radio One, Southern Sound, Norwich Radio and Radio Leeds. I have always had a good response and only a few troublemakers. Sometimes the trouble comes

from within, as happened to me when I made a –
guest appearance on the BBC's local radio station in
Exeter.

The disc jockey handling our interview was all
smarm and charm when I arrived. He told me we
were going to have a really smashing afternoon and
have lots of fun with the listeners. I was encouraged
to 'make myself at home' in the big studio.

Then he went on air: 'Today, I've got with me
Keith Charles the psychic policeman. He is appearing
at St George's Hall, in Exeter,' he told his listeners.

Then the bombshell: 'Now then, Keith, tell me,
what is your view on the Immaculate Conception?'
This DJ then leapt up out of his seat, walked across
the studio and began sorting out records, leaving me
to answer a question that had very little relevance to
clairvoyance! He went on to attack me in every way
possible. 'Catholics wouldn't believe all this.' ...
'What do you say to Catholics who do this, and do
that?'

Placed in an intolerable situation over which I could
so easily have lost total control, I was most
uncomfortable for some ten minutes. I knew I had to
fight back or I would have had little credibility with
the people of Exeter. I gave my view about the
Immaculate Conception, for what it was worth, and
when the DJ told me I'd probably just offended every
Catholic in the county, I added: 'Sorry, but you asked
me along to give my opinions. That is my opinion. If

it doesn't fall in line with what you would have liked me to say, that is your problem. Not mine! Perhaps you should have asked me a more relevant question!'

I went on, 'If my response offends Catholics then that is their problem – not mine. I have expressed a personal opinion!'

I believe honesty is necessary. I believe people respect it, even if they do not necessarily agree. You won't find me pulling any punches in this book and I appreciate that some of the views I express here are controversial.

When the film *Ghost* hit the big screen, I didn't give it much thought. I am not a cinemagoer but when a friend told me the film was about a clairvoyant and was worth seeing, I took an evening off to take a look. I wasn't disappointed. The storyline was about a medium and life after death. Off-screen, the star, Patrick Swayze, related a personal spiritual experience. He revealed that a surfing accident left him on the verge of drowning. He thought he was a goner when, suddenly, an ancient warrior rose up out of the water in front of him. This warrior was covered in body paint and carried a sword in his right hand. Said Swayze: 'He just grabbed hold of me, told me not to panic, and reassured me we would make it to safety – which we did.'

Of course, this could have been a primed publicity story to push the film but I tend to think not. More likely the warrior was Patrick's own spirit guide who came to his rescue in response to Patrick's psychic call for help.

My own 'doorman', as we call our guides, is a Mongolian warrior.

So, the film *Ghost* did a great deal to create interest about life after death, and Patrick Swayze's own personal experience made it doubly effective.

I am all for drawing attention to life after death in this, or any other, way. It makes people curious and curious people think, then draw conclusions.

Now I am doing my best to encourage everyone associated with clairvoyance to be much more open about their belief, even controversial. Let the world take a long, hard look at us and be influenced by our sincerity in what we know to be true.

It bugs me a little that Stephen O'Brien has labelled himself 'successor' to Doris Stokes. Why does there need to be a successor? Is clairvoyance a competition in which we must be as good, or better, than the next one? It's just not on! Maybe former television sports presenter David Icke saw himself in such a role.

When he popped up from nowhere with his prophecies of doom and gloom, he was labelled as just another spiritualist nutter. Icke is not a spiritualist and he is not a clairvoyant. In fact, I am not sure what he is, though he certainly wrote and publicised his book. You can't take that away from him.

However, I don't feel able to say for certain that

his so-called messages from God were definitely not from God. Nobody can, any more than anyone can prove the messages I receive are not from spirit. The only difference, perhaps, is that my messages have credibility because they can be double-checked by those receiving them.

The David Ickes of this world don't help the cause of spiritualism or the people who believe in 'the spirit world'. They give spiritualism a bad name but, then, so do mediums who go rushing off to newspapers claiming they have spoken to Winston Churchill who has told them he is having an affair in Heaven with Ava Gardner!

Then there are women who claim their dead husbands make love to them. I know how very hard it is to communicate with the dead, never mind make love to them! What good do these kind of claims do? These liars just make us all look like idiots. Life after death – great! Sex after death – terrific.

Having said that, I repeat that if people are at least discussing something, it is better than ignoring it, whatever conclusions they draw. More and more, life after death and the work of mediums like me are being put under the spotlight. That is encouraging and healthy.

Quite often, I sit down with people who say they don't believe in ghosts but want to know what I think.

All ghosts are spirits. They are the vibrations of the

person who has passed over and it is not unusual for me to spend an hour or more discussing these points. So who is the silly one, talking for an hour about something they do not believe in?

The Spiritualist Church is in religion's third division. Anyone can call him- or herself a spiritualist and start regular meetings and services. It is so amateurish and so unprofessional, unlike religions such as the Church of England and the Roman Catholic Church where there is much more regulation. Nobody in Britain can practise as a priest unless he or she is qualified. Until spiritualism is similarly controlled, it will never be taken seriously.

There is still considerable personal prejudice, too, which largely comes from a lack of knowledge. For example, I have tried placing advertisements publicising my theatre appearances in several local newspapers and these were apparently refused because of the personal prejudice of the editor or his or her management. I phone in with my advertisement, to be told that it will cost £100. Then I get a letter, advising me: 'Sorry, we cannot take your ad because the editor will not accept it.' Then another paper in the same town will accept the same ad without question.

It is the same with some theatres. Around twenty-five per cent of British theatres and town halls will not take our bookings, through prejudice. They tell us, 'We don't have spiritualism here.' It's like saying,

'We don't allow 'flu here!' or, 'We don't have dirty kitchens in our town hall!'

Apart from a vociferous section of the Born Again Christians, nobody actually campaigns against the Spiritualist Church. It is almost solely personal prejudice that is giving spiritualism a bad name, and perhaps the movement has only itself to blame. Fearing such reaction, in the past followers have tended to keep to themselves and have met in secret.

As I have already indicated, television is biased in that it consistently takes a negative attitude to spiritualism. Many invitations are extended to certain religious TV programmes to show meetings. They are always declined. My view is that this is a particularly serious area of prejudice because of the power of television. Fortunately, most national newspapers and the overseas press are much more open, fair-minded and tolerant. Perhaps this fair-mindedness will one day even be shown by those who control our television, although they still have some way to go.

Again, if mediums want to be taken seriously, they must be seen to be competent at what they do. Many are not. It is no use trying to persuade television to bring its cameras into spiritualist churches if the mediums they show are poorly trained. The general standard of mediumship is poor and I put this down to the fact that there aren't sufficient people qualified to train others to a high standard. Mediumship is not just about being able to say, 'Hello, I've got your dad here . . .' This is only a part of it. More important is being able to pass on accurate and meaningful messages.

A medium once said to me that I was reading books on the occult. 'You have such a book by your bed,' he told me.

I answered: 'No, the only book I have on my bedside table is the Bible.'

To this he replied: 'If you were clairvoyant, you would be able to see what I mean!' This medium was not only mischievous, he was totally inaccurate.

The same medium then told a woman in the audience, 'You have had a row with your husband and he has gone off and left you.'

The woman said, 'No, we just had a row over dinner before coming to church.'

The man then said: 'That's what you think. He is having an affair!' This was absolutely dreadful. It had nothing to do with mediumship and the message was total rubbish.

I was present in a spiritualist church when a medium told a woman in the hall that they (the medium and the woman) had been married in Atlantis! He then informed her that he intended to communicate with her without speaking. He put his hand on his head, didn't say a word, then asked her: 'Did you understand that?' The woman looked at the medium, lost for words. She hadn't a clue what he was talking about!

It was totally outrageous behaviour and, afterwards, I protested strongly to those in charge. I was told there was little they could do when they needed a medium on their platform four times a week, fifty-two weeks each year. They couldn't be choosey! No wonder it is so easy to give spiritualism a bad name. This type of medium should be expelled from our movement.

CHAPTER TEN

DEAD SOCCER STAR IS MY SPIRIT GUIDE

Sport was always one of my passions when I was a kid. I played rugby for Brighton and for my school and I was hot stuff on the soccer field, with a regular place in the Brighton Boys' Club team.

My hero was always Scottish soccer international John White, who wore the Number 8 shirt for Tottenham Hotspurs. I followed his career in the newspapers and on the radio and TV.

Then, on 21 July 1964, John White was playing

golf at Crews Hill Golf Club in Middlesex when a bad storm stopped play. John sheltered under an oak tree which was hit by lightning and he died. He was only about twenty-eight.

Although I came to terms with not seeing John White and that figure eight blazoned across his back, I always felt he hadn't quite left my life. It was as though, somehow, he was with me, but I put this feeling down to his memory being so etched on my young mind. I'd be sitting watching the Saturday-afternoon football on television and I'd have this idea I wasn't in the room alone, yet I knew I was.

Thankfully, it wasn't my mind playing tricks, as I was to discover a number of years later when well-known medium Bill Marie came round to our house for a chat. He said he was picking up very strong psychic vibes, then turned to me and began telling me how I had always had a passion for sport, especially soccer. Then he asked if I was aware that a spirit named John White worked very closely with me?

I told him how I'd often felt that someone else was in the same room with me when I was watching football on television but, as a kid, I had no idea why or what it was all about. I wasn't aware of being psychic when I was a small boy, even though I was just beginning to experience what seemed like weird happenings.

'John White is the dead soccer player you idolised.

He has been working closely with you for a long time,' Bill told me.

This made sense because, as I say, even though I was alone I had often felt someone was sitting alongside me on our sofa when football was being shown on the television.

For some reason, though, John White's spirit has never made itself known to me clairvoyantly. As a spirit helper, it doesn't really need to. Besides, it is good enough for me to know he is around.

In this way, soccer star John White was my first spirit celebrity. After I became seriously involved in clairvoyance, from about the age of thirty-one, I became more and more involved with showbusiness people. We just seemed to gravitate towards each other. I think they liked my laid-back style, my youthfulness and exuberance, not to mention my cheeky sense of humour which helps to put people at ease. That's how I became known as 'Psychic to the Stars', a name given to me by one of the Sunday newspapers. It has caught on.

This side of my psychic work just snowballed. I'd meet people at celebrity events and they would be so fascinated that I was a psychic policeman that they'd invite me for a drink or a meal.

This is what happened when I first met American actress Leigh Taylor-Young. She wanted to know more and asked me to dinner at her London hotel. Over the pudding course, I gave her a reading. Her grandfather came through and was telling her that when she arrived back in the States she should travel south to sign some important contracts.

She told me that she'd only found out about the contracts that same morning. She was impressed that I knew about them and very impressed that I knew they had to be signed as a matter of urgency.

Before I left her, Leigh game me a book entitled *One Way Out*. She wrote inside the cover: 'To Keith. Spirit arranges things beautifully.' She also gave me her American address and asked me to keep in touch.

Sometimes, people need to know something important to them from beyond the grave. Ever since his death, the unanswered question has always been, did champion boxer Freddie Mills commit suicide or was he killed? Crimewriters and others have been speculating over that one ever since and still the mystery remains unsolved.

However, the one person who probably wanted to know the truth more than anyone else was Freddie's wife. She came to me and Bob Brunton for a private reading at Wimbledon Church. Freddie came through to us that day and told his wife, through me, what really happened.

When Freddie died I was only an eight-year-old kid, so when this boxer came through and talked about clubs and boxing and gave birthday dates, Mrs Mills was impressed. She knew it must be Freddie.

The details of that conversation with Mrs Freddie

Mills must remain confidential. It was a very private matter. All I can say is that Mrs Mills went away a much happier woman, knowing what really happened to her husband.

Another boxer who came my way was Duke McKenzie. He was with a girl who I believe was his sister-in-law. It was a relative of hers who came through in spirit.

I was urged to go to the man sitting next to the girl because the spirit message was that if this man was a mechanic he would be the best there is. Spirit added, to be a good mechanic he must work hard and within two years he would reach the top.

What a strange message, especially as that man happened to be Duke McKenzie, hardly a mechanic!

Two years later Duke McKenzie won the European Championship and, during his fight, commentator Harry Carpenter said, 'Duke McKenzie is doing a real mechanic's job here tonight.' I was looking in, and when I heard Harry use that word 'mechanic' I nearly fell off my seat!

Duke went on to punch his way into British boxing history by being crowned world champion for the third time. Spirit certainly knew he was a winner.

When you have experienced so many incidents like this, little snippets of information which only make sense if they are true, then you will forgive me for having no doubt that they come from spirit, from beyond the grave.

Another showbusiness story involved British comedian Bernie Clifton. Normally, one pays to see this man and he is worth every penny as he is a very funny performer. I'd booked a Newquay theatre called the Cosy Nook. It is right on the seafront and holds about six hundred people.

Before the evening performance, Derek Robinson, our road show manager, told me to go backstage where someone wanted to talk to me. It was Bernie Clifton who was starring in his own show the following day. He asked if he could come in and watch our psychic evening. In return, he happily agreed to draw the raffle ticket prizes.

During the clairvoyance, a fireman named Johnson came through and nobody laid claim to him at first! However, I felt this one was for Bernie and in the end he agreed he had known a fireman who passed over but he couldn't be sure of his name.

However, ex-fireman Johnson seemed to know all about Bernie Clifton. He told him, through me, that Bernie had just opened a new bank account but not in his own name of Bernie Clifton. Bernie agreed that was true. Johnson said Bernie was just about to go off to Spain to work. Again spirit Johnson was spot on. Afterwards Bernie told me he was amazed when I told him about the new bank account because absolutely nobody knew about it, apart from the bank!

I am quite used to the snipers of this world taking verbal potshots at mediums. When I am on tour, if it isn't the Born Again Christians, with their banners and their heckling, making mischief, it's probably a lonely drunk who has found his way into our audience with a half-full bottle of Scotch, wanting to make a point or two. That's OK, they can all have their say. We don't mind.

The drunk will usually slink away but the so-called Christians sometimes like to use violence, stabbing their banners at us or lashing out with their hands.

We've had some of that treatment even in a nice place like Norwich. Right in the middle of message-giving, a man stood up during a meeting and began shouting out that we'd got it all wrong. It was reported that he was a member of a well-known pop group, but I cannot vouch for that.

What he didn't take into account was the fact that he made his protest to some five hundred converted people. Nobody in the audience wanted to hear what he had to say. They were just irritated that he had so rudely interrupted their meeting. He was soon howled down.

Strangely enough, some months later I was giving clairvoyance at a meeting in Ramsgate and this same guy walked up to me and asked, 'Keith Charles?' I told him I remembered him from Norwich. This time, however, he didn't make a fuss.

We had another of our occasional upsets with people who believe they are closer to God than ourselves when we held a meeting at Taunton in Somerset.

Our evening of clairvoyance was described as 'wickedness' by elders of the Octagon Chapel at East Reach. Pamphlets were handed around outside the theatre, protesting at our presence, but the meeting still went ahead to a full house. In fact, Jessie Nason and I, both now internationally known, went down so well that we were booked for the following year.

I can cope with the James Randis of this world and the banner-waving Born Again Christians when I hear stories like the one told by Katie Boyle about her dead husband Greville.

She has had proof that her husband is keeping an eye on her from the spirit world. He even used parking meters to make the point!

Katie's husband died suddenly at 4 a.m. in February 1976. Ten days later, and still in a state of shock, she was driving round London sorting out Greville's affairs. She recalled, 'Faces and voices blurred but what gradually became clear was that I was having no trouble finding parking meters. Very odd!' In fact, it was something Greville always stressed: 'Leave your car at home. You will never park!'

Continued Katie: 'When another parking space appeared at my next port of call, I said out loud, "Darling, are you helping me today?" Then I challenged him. "If you've got anything to do with this, then I'd like the next parking meter to be on the right." It was there!'

Coincidence? Katie tried again. She gave Greville full directions but, as she approached her next appointment, the place was packed. She said she gave a wry smile. 'Then I heard a toot – the driver of a parked car was leaving. I thanked him and backed into the space. As I looked up, I saw the number plate of the car in front. It read GPG – they were my husband's initials.'

Katie was right. It was no coincidence. It was spirit at work.

Our loved ones have most ingenious ways of letting us know they aren't as far away as we might imagine and that they certainly aren't gone for ever.

There is no one better qualified to verify that than the romantic novelist Barbara Cartland. Dame Barbara has given me her own truly moving account of the way her husband Hugh found a way to prove to her he was in spirit:

'My beloved husband, Hugh, died suddenly on December 29, 1963, one day after we had celebrated twenty-seven years of great happiness.

'He was a quiet person who hated publicity, and, having loved me for eight years before we were married, he was the most contented man I have ever known.

'Once I said to him: "If a fairy could wave a magic wand and give you anything you wanted, what would you wish to have?"

'Hugh thought for a moment, and replied: "I have everything I have ever wanted."

'He loved me deeply but he believed that death was the end of everything; there was no afterlife, no meeting in another world with those we loved.

'After his death I had a message which told me he had been mistaken. I have written down exactly what happened so that it will help other people.

'On July 31, 1917, at the Third Battle of Ypres, 2nd Lieut. Hugh McCorquodale received the Military Cross – "for his gallantry and devotion to duty during the action. It was largely due to his fine personal example and skilful handling of his Company that the enemy counter-attack was delayed."

'My husband was just nineteen years old when he was posted to the 6th Battalion in Flanders. Two months later came the terrible slaughter at Passchendaele.

'In this battle the expectation of a subaltern's life was twenty minutes. On July 31 there were 279 casualties in the battalion, and Hugh was severely – almost mortally – wounded.

'In attacking the enemy trenches he was hit with a sniper's dum-dum bullet which passed right through his right shoulder and out of his back, exploding as it went. This, among other injuries, collapsed his lung and smashed three ribs. He turned head over heels and lay out in no-man's land for forty-eight hours.

' "You were very near to death," I said to him when we married. "Did you see angels, hear voices, or even feel you were being helped or sustained?"

' "No," he replied, "I just felt very tired and far away from all the noise of the battle."

'During the second night Hugh was carried in on a man's back and received a number of shrapnel wounds in the process. At the field dressing station, they treated only the shrapnel wounds, not realising he was injured elsewhere.

'He was carried down to the base, but the shelling was so bad that the stretcher-bearers dropped him continually, and when he eventually arrived at No 9 Red Cross Hospital at Calais he was so covered in mud they did not realise he was an officer and he was at first put in the Tommies' ward.

'When the doctors examined Hugh they said there was nothing they could do and there wasn't a chance of his survival. He was, therefore, as was the practice in those days, put outside in a tent in the grounds of the hospital by himself to die.

'On August 25, his uncle, General Lord Home of Stirkoke, who was commanding the First Army, was informed and he sent for Hugh's parents to come over from England to say "Goodbye" to their son. Mr and Mrs Harold McCorquodale crossed the Channel and saw Hugh for what they thought was the last time.

'Hugh had fortunately been taken to a "rich" hospital which was run by the Canadians, and they gave him port and champagne when they dressed his wounds, and the rest of the time he was under heroin.

'He lay for four weeks without food, in a state of semi-consciousness, and we now know that leaving him alone and letting him get over the shock was what saved his life.

'After attending five hospitals and having innumerable operations, Hugh survived.

'He was a "show piece" for the doctors, as they considered it a tremendous achievement that they had kept him alive, and he remembered being constantly "shown off" to visiting specialists.

'When he was discharged the doctors told him: "It is a miracle you are alive. Nothing more can be done by surgery, so never let anyone fiddle about with you. You must trust to nature and live with your disability."

'It was advice he was to stick to all his life and gave him what amounted to almost a fear of doctors.

'Hugh was listed as 40 per cent disabled and

received a pension which, at the time of his death, was £185.16s a year!

'His convalescence was very slow and when I met him first, in 1927, I was told by various members of his family, including his mother, that he wasn't expected to live long and if he ever got influenza he would die.

'We often talked about "the afterlife". He didn't believe in one.

'He was a very quiet, gentle man, who never forced his opinions on anyone, but if I asked him what he thought, he always told me the truth.

'On December 29, 1963, after two days of slight bronchitis, Hugh got out of bed and collapsed. The scar tissues from the terrible wounds he had received in 1917 had touched his heart.

'I had always known Hugh's life hung on a thread and I was deeply grateful for having had him with me for so long.

'He did not suffer and for him it was the peaceful, quick death he would have wanted. But that did not assuage the ghastly shock and the terrible sense of loss.

'I had never seen anyone dead before – all my family had died in France. As I stood beside him as he lay in a blue bed wearing blue pyjamas, I could not believe when he had loved me so much that he had left me alone.

'A week after the funeral my maid, who had

been with me for over twenty-five years said: "Have you noticed the wonderful scent of carnations outside Mr McCorquodale's dressing room?"

' "No," I replied. "Are you sure? There haven't been any carnations in the house since the funeral and those in the wreaths had no fragrance, not in December."

' "I was so surprised at the strength of the perfume," my maid went on, "that I called the daily woman and drew her attention to it. She smelt it too but said it must be something someone had put in the bath."

'I didn't think any more about this conversation, but the next morning I got up at 8 o'clock as usual to give my son Glen his breakfast before leaving for London. There is an entresol with only a skylight outside my bedroom, on to which opened the doors from my husband's dressing room, his bathroom and the room in which he died.

'As I crossed the entresol I was suddenly aware of the marvellous, almost overpowering, scent of carnations. It was unlike any carnations I had ever smelt in England – it was the true exotic fragrance of Malmaisons which I hadn't known for years.

'I stood for a moment feeling astounded, then had to hurry downstairs in case Glen missed his train. When he had gone, I came upstairs and the scent was still there but fainter.

'I thought I must have imagined it but the following morning it was there again. It was, I discovered, in patches, the strongest scent being next to my husband's dressing room. Some mornings it wasn't there at all, or I couldn't smell it until I returned upstairs after breakfast.

'The fragrance came and went for three weeks. I asked a friend of mine who had been a medium if she noticed anything, not saying what I was thinking.

'She identified the unmistakable scent of Malmaison carnations and found it all round my bedroom door.

'I then knew exactly why it was there. My husband and I had always bought red carnations when we went abroad. Every year we went to Paris for a "second honeymoon". The first thing we would do on arrival was to drive to the Madeleine. Outside, there are always rows of colourful flower stalls.

'Hugh would buy me a huge bunch of red carnations before we went into church and said a prayer for our marriage. This was something we had done on our first honeymoon and repeated every year except during the war.

'The carnations would be arranged in my bedroom.

'Each evening when we went out to dinner Hugh would wear one in his buttonhole.

'If anything was a symbol of our happiness and our closeness to each other, it was red carnations. Now I understand why the scent of them was near my door. It could only mean one thing, that Hugh was trying to tell me he had been wrong.

'He had found a way to convey to me the truth – there is an afterlife; there is survival after death.'

Dame Barbara Cartland's experience is, of course, very special to her, but is the kind of spirit communication which many people have experienced after the loss of a loved one.

There is no doubt that the strong earthly bond of love 'pulls' spirit back to reassure those they have left behind that there is another dimension of life to look forward to; that there will be a reunion of our souls.

Sometimes spirit returns to us for other reasons, as it did with Genesis star Phil Collins. In his case, it was to give him a warning that could well have saved the lives of his three children, Joely, Simon and Lily.

Phil says his late father warned him that a pair of old electric blankets he planned to put in his kids' bedrooms were potential killers.

'Night after night the blankets we'd stored under our bed were mysteriously scattered around the bedroom floor. It was scary; I couldn't work it out.

Eventually, a medium told me it was a warning from my father not to use the electric blankets because the wiring was faulty and they would catch fire if they were used,' Phil told an American radio phone-in.

Is it all just coincidence? Is there some simple earthly explanation for happenings like these, as some will have us believe? Through my spirit-given knowledge, I know that we all live on. That there is life after life.

CHAPTER ELEVEN

MY PSYCHIC CHILDREN

I have been married twice, the first time to Maureen who was a nurse when I first met her, and now to Christine, who is a government administration officer.

A detective constable named Bob Winter was with me the night I first set eyes on Maureen. Not so long after that, poor old Bob died. At his funeral I had one of my most remarkable visions.

I'd been on night duty and hadn't had much sleep on the day of the funeral. I was standing in the church looking around me, as you do on such occasions, as Bob's body was reverently carried in and set down at the altar.

I said quietly to myself, 'If there is life after death, show me a sign.'

Almost immediately, an image of Bob's face appeared to me quite clearly against one of the pastel-coloured walls of the church, but the face was wearing eye patches!

I muttered, 'What are you doing wearing eye patches?'

I heard him say, 'I am blind.'

Continuing this bizarre conversation with the vision showing like a colour slide projection on the church wall, I pointed out that he was not blind.

'I am now,' Bob told me. Then the image disappeared.

The funeral service was not disturbed and, as far as I was aware, nobody else had seen the image of Bob Winter's face on the wall. That was for my eyes only.

A few minutes later, I knew why. In his address, the vicar told how compassionate Bob had been, even to the point of donating his organs to help others. I learned later that his eyes had been donated after his passing into spirit, as he had wanted. There was my proof.

It was remarkable, but just another example of clear evidence given to me that there is life after death. How else could my vision be explained? I had no idea at all that Bob Winter had bequeathed his eyes in this way.

Dear old Bob would want me to know he was all right in his new spirit world. We shared many interesting, and often comical, moments together, one of them being on the night I first met the nurse who became my wife and mother of my three sons.

Bob and I had been called out to St George's Hospital in Tooting in response to a fellow who swore blind he had been robbed and thrown into the lake on Wimbledon Common. When we arrived at the hospital, it was as much as we could do to keep a straight face.

This bloke looked just like Buster Keaton, the silent movie star. He was wearing a white hospital gown, which did up at the back, over which was a plastic packamac. Soaking wet shoes, on his otherwise bare feet, squelched as he walked along the corridor. His hair was dripping and bedraggled, hanging to one side of his gnarled old face. What a sight!

There were two nurses on duty. One was six feet tall, blonde and leggy, an absolutely gorgeous girl named Kathy. The other one was Maureen, dark-haired, petite and very attractive.

Maureen told us we would have to take the little fellow home because there was no reason to keep him in hospital. We soon established the fact that he had not been robbed at all. So what he was doing taking a dip in a Wimbledon Common pond was anyone's guess. He'd probably ridden into it in the dark on his bicycle!

Bob called up Tooting Bec police station and a strapping six feet four inches tall copper came along in a van to take the little guy, and his bike, back home. It was the funniest sight, the tall copper and the little Buster Keaton chap, still in his hospital gown and wheeling his bike, walking together to the police van.

Bob and I stayed on a bit longer, at Maureen's invitation, to have a cup of coffee. She and I seemed to hit it off, so I called back later and asked her if she'd like a night out at the London Palladium. She accepted. One thing led to another and we began to see quite a lot of each other. We were married on 7 July 1973.

It is a strange thing, but Maureen is related to Sir Arthur Conan Doyle. Her grandfather's name was Doyle and through him there was a family link with Sir Arthur Conan Doyle who was a spiritualist. Maureen eventually became a spiritualist, too, like Sir Arthur and like me.

A few years on, when I was about thirty-one, I still hadn't developed my gift as a medium. In fact, at that point I had had nothing at all to do with spiritualism. I hardly knew what a medium was.

Maureen was doing a bit of part-time nursing. When one of the patients died, she and an auxiliary nurse named Rosina were laying out the dead patient ready for removal to the mortuary. Maureen said thoughtfully, 'I wonder where she is now?' The two of them began discussing life after death. Maureen told Rosina about her own psychic experiences and said her husband (that was me) experienced them too.

The outcome of all that was that Rosina invited me to go and talk to her, which I did. After I had recounted some of my psychic experiences, she said I had better become a medium.

Then, as we talked, a strange thing happened. I was aware of another woman in the room with us, only at first she wasn't visible. I felt cold and shivery. Then, suddenly, I could 'see' the spirit woman, which was what she was, and she spoke reassuringly to me. As suddenly as she had appeared to me, she was gone and I was back with Rosina. Rosina understood what I had just experienced and asked me to go away and draw the face of the woman I had seen in the room with us.

At the time I had no idea that Rosina's father was a medium named Percy Webster and that her mother had also been a powerful medium. Nor did she tell me.

When I left I promised to try to draw the face I'd seen. I was working in the fraud squad in Holborn at the time and, a few days later, on duty with a bit of time to kill, I tried to sketch the face. I managed to draw one side but there was no way I could seem to draw the right-hand side of the woman's face. I made three different sketches but in each case I failed miserably. In the end I had to give up.

When I told Rosina, she just smiled, and said to me, 'That is all I wanted to know.' Then she told me that the woman I had seen was her dead mother. Her mother had suffered from palsy. As a result, she would never allow her picture to be taken showing the right side of her face. Rosina knew there was no way I was going to be able to draw it. She was convinced I was good medium material. She told me bluntly that I should seek the right kind of help to develop my gift.

Rosina also confided that, after her mother had died, she sat with another medium (not her father) who told her that a complete stranger would bring her dead mother's spirit to her. Two years on, I was that stranger.

I have Maureen to thank for introducing me to Rosina, who, in turn, opened the door for me into spiritualism. The next step was to take up an invitation from Rosina's father, Percy Webster, to see him at work as a medium at Hampton Hill Spiritualist Church in Middlesex.

The year was 1980, and this was the very first time I had even seen a clairvoyant in action. Webster gave out messages. Then he announced to the fifty-or-so people in the small hall that his friend, Keith, was going to pass on some messages.

I froze. I said to Maureen, 'How am I going to do that?'

I went to the front, alongside Percy, and stared hard at the faces looking expectantly in my direction, all waiting for me to say something stunning!

There was a woman in the front row and, for some reason I cannot explain, I was drawn to her. I told her that her mother, Dorothy, was telling me how much her daughter had loved her home-baked cakes. 'Oh, yes. That's right,' she confirmed.

We had quite a little chat, the three of us – me, Dorothy and her daughter! I was a bit bemused. Nothing like this had ever happened to me before and I could not explain it. But I knew I wanted to do it again.

If you like, that was my baptism into clairvoyance. From there I took Rosina and her father, Percy's, advice, and joined a spiritualist church to seek psychic development. On Rosina's advice, I was introduced to the Kingston Spiritualist Church where I joined a development circle in Crawley, under medium Berenice Watt.

In these circles an experienced medium helps you to explore your psychic ability and its potential. There is a great deal to learn and serious, meaningful discussion takes place.

I was living in Chessington at the time, however, and Crawley was a long way to travel. Then I discovered a medium living in Chessington who took

'circles'. I found out that I could attend her development classes if I liked. On my first visit, however, she
told me, 'There is very little I can teach you. You are
a natural clairvoyant!' She began telling me that she
could see me giving demonstrations in big halls, with
people queuing for tickets to my shows.

I didn't know what she was on about. I didn't even
know how to become a medium and here she was
telling me I was going to be a famous psychic. I didn't
believe a word of it!

However, the more she taught me, the more I
realised that this ex-circus trapeze artiste, named
Madge Summerfield, knew what it was all about.

The word 'circle' is a bit old-fashioned because it
does tend to conjure up pictures of a group of people
sitting around a table, touching hands and holding a
seance. About eight of us did sit around a table, in
what Madge called her sanctuary, but there was no
seance.

She would start with a prayer, then she would teach
us how to relax, how to open our minds to our
psychic powers, how to meditate – and how to link
with spirit.

We had to learn how to ask spirit to come closer to
us. We would practise on each other. I might face
Eric, so I would say, 'Spirit come and speak to me.
Tell me something about Eric.' I might pick up the
fact that he had a new pair of shoes at home – little
things like that.

I soon got very bored. I became restless and wanted to get out into big halls and do it, not learn about it! I lasted about three months, then I told Madge I was off to see if I could get a church booking.

At Tolworth Church in Surrey I joined Percy Webster. They checked me out, knew I was ready and asked what name I wanted to use. I told them 'Keith Charles'. The Charles was after my grandad, whose spirit was the first I saw and which I recognised. Also, I had to keep my own name of Wright private as this is the name I use in my work as a police officer, which has always come first in my career.

My second demonstration of clairvoyance was at Hampton Spiritualist Church. It was a memorable occasion because there were only four people in the audience, and one of those was the organist!

The youngest was about sixty-five and I think he was the one who called out that I was talking a load of rubbish!

On the way home in my car, I had to ask myself a serious question. What was I doing? That evening I had managed to pack in an audience of just four people and there I was, a young whipper-snapper pushing on thirty-one, telling these old fogies all about survival after death. They didn't need a preacher like me. They knew it all already. They were the converted.

The thought of coming straight off police night duty, tarting myself up in my best suit and confronting a hall full of little old ladies wasn't really what I had in mind. Besides, as far as they were concerned, I was much too young. How could I possibly know about such things as life after death?

However, I knew I was breaking new ground, that it was necessary for someone like me to shake things up a little, or even a lot. Spiritualism was crusty, old-fashioned, boring, tedious. It needed a new audience, new blood, new motivation. I would be the psychic crusader to bring clairvoyance in Britain into the twenty-first century. I believed I could do that because I have such powerful motivation.

Over the past ten years, I believe I have achieved quite a bit of this early aim and my meetings round the country prove it. The average age of my audiences is now around thirty-five, not sixty-five as it was when I first started out.

Maureen wasn't too sure what to make of it all. She had an open mind about me becoming seriously involved. If that was what I wanted to do, it was OK with her. As I remember, after she had had some interesting chats with Rosina and Percy about life after death, Maureen decided to investigate spiritual-ism herself.

So here I was, a full-time policeman, with a home to keep and a part-time job as an increasingly active psychic.

Three children had already come along and cer-tainly one of them, Mathew, was showing all the signs of also having the psychic gift.

Mathew Charles, the eldest of my sons, was born on 20 March 1974; Daniel James on 17 July 1975 and, finally, Michael John on 20 March 1978, which, as you will have noticed, was on the same day as Mathew, only four years apart.

We lost one boy in between, who would have been named Philip. Philip has been in touch, and psychic artist Coral Polge drew a spirit picture of him. Mathew saw the picture and told me he had seen Philip in his bedroom several times.

Tragically, on 16 November 1994, as this book was being prepared for publication, we lost Mathew to spirit as the result of a fatal road accident. Our tribute to him follows at the end of this chapter.

Mathew took after me, only I would say he was more psychically aware than I was at his age. He had numerous experiences and wanted to develop. He first started showing signs of being able to communicate with spirit when he was around seven. He could have become super-psychic had he lived. One time he sat with medium Madge Summerfield and communicated with Madge's dead mother. He passed on some incredible information, so Madge told me.

Mathew also gave my mum, his grandmother, a reading in her kitchen and told her things about herself, and her past, that he could not possibly have known. Mum was stunned. He told her that he had her grandfather, Albert, with him. Albert was telling my boy things about the family, about my mum's sister and how she had died.

Mathew said he believed her name was 'Mavis' although he thought he hadn't got this quite right. (In fact, it was Iris.) Then he said he could see her on a bike, riding fast and hitting lumps of metal – precisely what caused the accident which killed her. (Iris was killed by a wartime bomb in Brighton.)

He told my mum about the wooden doll she had as a little girl, but how many kids of seventeen would even know about wooden dolls? She did have a wooden doll, although it really belonged to her sister.

Then came the day when one of Mathew's psychic predictions matched one of mine. I could have cashed in when I told Maureen I had just had a psychic feeling that Spurs were going to lose their Cup Final match against Coventry three goals to two.

'That's funny,' said Maureen. 'A few days ago Mathew told me the same thing.' I went straight off to the local bookie and laid out £2 for 40–1 odds on Coventry beating Spurs 3–2.

Spurs lost 3–2 in extra time but I didn't get a penny because the betting shop result had to be the result at full time, in ninety minutes, not the extra-time result.

When Mathew was at school, a new teacher from Australia joined the staff. One day in class, this teacher asked Mathew's class what they thought he did before he came to Britain. Mathew asked spirit, who gave him the answer. 'You were a train driver,'

Mathew told his new teacher. The guy apparently nearly fell flat on his back and wanted to know how my boy knew. 'Because I am psychic,' he said.

So Mathew was psychic and very interested in life after death; Daniel can take it or leave it; and Michael doesn't really want to know. That's fine. I certainly wouldn't try to put anything in their heads but if it is there already it is up to them if they want to know more about it. I will always help.

Let me tell you of another incident concerning my family and its very psychic links.

Maureen woke in the early hours one night and sat up in bed absolutely startled, having seen an Indian in a bright blue head-dress standing at the end of our bed. I asked her why she didn't wake me up but she said it was the most incredible thing that had ever happened to her and she just froze.

The next time she saw our psychic friend Madge Summerfield, even before Maureen had a chance to open her mouth, Madge told Maureen she had seen her spirit guide. Maureen said that was why she had come to see Madge.

Then, on one of our visits to see psychic artist Coral Polge, Coral drew a number of pictures, including one of an Indian. We took them home and Maureen laid them out on the dining room table.

Mathew came home from school, saw the Indian picture and calmly announced that he was the Indian he sometimes saw standing at the top of the stairs.

'He's often here,' said Mathew.

His psychic eye revealed itself when Mathew was only nine. One of the first instances was when my wife's great-aunt had been in hospital for an operation on a brain tumour. She said that, in hospital, she saw a Roman soldier stop at the bottom of her bed and she told him to clear off because she wasn't ready to go with him just yet!

The aunt was over eighty but made a full recovery. A walking miracle was the way the hospital described her. Anyway, some ten years after the aunt died, Maureen and Mathew went to see the old lady's daughter who was about to emigrate to Australia.

When they left the house, Mathew asked his mother, 'Why was that Roman soldier standing by the chair?' He didn't know the story but I explained to him that what he saw was a spirit guide.

One thing I warned Mathew not to do was experiment with the ouija board. We have all probably played the ouija board game, but I have to say that it is to be avoided. It can be dangerous. A gun isn't dangerous if it is handled properly, but use it badly and it is lethal.

Soon after singer Freddie Mercury died, Mathew was telling me how he and some friends adapted a pack of playing cards to represent an ouija board. They made the red ace 'Yes' and the black ace 'No'.

When they began playing, they believed they had made contact with Freddie Mercury's spirit. 'If you really are Freddie Mercury, give us a sign,' said Mathew. He produced a card. When he looked at the card, he saw it was a queen. Freddie's band was called Queen. Coincidence? Maybe . . . maybe not.

People dabble with the ouija board mostly out of curiosity. Pretend for a moment that we are spirits over on the other side looking in on a bunch of drunken idiots playing the ouija board. They've had too much to drink, they don't know what they are doing and they want to get in touch!

These spirits say, 'Let's have a game with them.' Spirit spells out a name one of the idiots will know and, before long, the earthly idiots are dead worried.

Now, to be serious for a moment, the danger here is that they may get hold of aggressive spirits, spirits who are fed up that they have died. So, when they are asked silly questions like, 'When will I die?' they might give the mischievous answer 'sixty-four'.

One of the idiots is sixty-three, so now they believe they're going to snuff it the following year!

The people I know use the ouija board for sensible purposes, not as a game. You wouldn't give a gun to an eight-year-old, say, 'Here are some bullets. Go and play with it!' Neither would you give your car keys to a ten-year-old and say, 'Go and take a spin.'

The ouija board is used by some spiritualists to create a link to the spirit world. Much of the evidence obtained about life after death at the Wimbledon Spiritualist Church came from using the ouija board.

I have used it about three times, once with a church minister and twice with other mediums.

On each occasion, we opened and closed with prayer. The ouija board is less demanding because you pool your psychic and spiritual energy. If there are five of you in a circle using fifty per cent of this energy, then you have two hundred and fifty per cent energy level in use, which is greater than one hundred per cent of one person's efforts.

As mediums, we use the ouija board to ask those who have passed over to describe their new world. In fact, I have been in touch with a medium named Bob Brunton, a member of my church who died.

So the board has its uses but it is not my favourite way of communicating. There is always the element of doubt.

As for the danger of becoming obsessed through use of the ouija board, I don't think this is possible. We all have our own spirit guides looking after us and I have never heard of anyone being 'taken over'.

Some mediums claim it is a way of finding out about the future but I am doubtful. Even clairvoyants don't always know what is in store for them.

I didn't know that my marriage to Maureen would end in March 1992 with a divorce. We had a reasonably happy life together but, after twenty years or more, we had both changed. Time changes everyone, it doesn't matter who it is. Maureen and I drifted apart.

Divorce is one of the worst things anyone can go through. It's like dealing with bereavement. Enormous emotions are disturbed and muddied. Enormous changes take place overnight.

Daniel and Michael still live with their mother and I'd hate to think our problems will rub off on to them. I am sure that is not what Maureen would want. I hope that time will heal her emotional hurt.

My second wife, Christine, has become interested in my work as a medium and is even quite psychic herself, something I hope to persuade her to develop further. She has, in fact, undertaken hypnotherapy regression through medium Ivor James. (This is the means by which people can explore their past lives.)

Christine's was especially interesting. She was able to recall vivid details of one of her past lives as a Red Indian squaw in her twenties, named Cherakia. She had to look after her ailing father and her family of three younger brothers and a sister, her mother having died.

Cherakia was able to recall living near mountains, spending her time cooking, washing and hunting rabbits which she fed to the family.

During the regression, Cherakia began to make exaggerated gestures and when Ivor asked her what she was doing, she told him she was drying out buffalo skins, stretching them to make tepees.

However, her good life as a squaw was not to last. Before she reached thirty, she drowned. Cherakia described in vivid detail how the men in her tribe and in a rival tribe were involved in a fight. She was dragged by the throat away from the fighting, was molested and thrown into a river where she drowned. To this day, Christine is terrified of water.

My own experience of regression revealed I have also lived before, as a Confederate soldier in the American Civil War. Maybe this is why I feel a very strong urge to go to America which could be my roots from a past life.

I was able to recall my death. We were in retreat but temporarily dug in behind a thick woodland, using cut-down trees as barricades.

I died when a cavalry officer charged me down and ran me through with his sword. It was a particularly violent and agonising death. I believe this explains my deep-felt fear of knives in this life.

Mathew

I had arrived in the CID office at Sutton at noon on Wednesday 16 November 1994 ready to face the day-to-day problems of the public.

Superintendent Ray Newark walked into the office as he often does and I caught his ear to discuss a theft, with a request that he write a letter to the loser as there was some delicacy regarding the nature of the complaint.

At 12.20 p.m. he put his head round the door and said, 'Keith, have you got a minute please in my office . . .' I didn't think anything was unusual at that stage as often he would discuss matters with officers. However, as we walked along the corridor to his office I was aware of my Detective Inspector Tony Kirkby, walking beside me with his head bowed to the floor.

'Come in Keith. Sit down,' said Ray Newark. 'No, I'm all right,' I said. Although, seeing my Detective Inspector there, and watching him shut the door, I thought to myself, 'Keith you are in the shit!' I thought someone had made a complaint against me.

Ray then put his arm on my shoulder and the words he spoke will be etched in my mind for ever, every parent's nightmare. 'Keith, there is no easy way of saying this. Your son Mathew was killed on his way to work this morning. I am sorry to have to tell you this.'

My legs turned to jelly, my stomach turned over, and tears filled my eyes . . . 'Don't tell me this, please.'

I turned and saw a wooden cupboard. I wanted to punch it, but I thought if I did I would damage it. I saw an old metal radiator and kicked it several times.

I remember looking out of the window and seeing people in the high street, waiting at the bus stop, and going about their normal lives. Strange maybe, but I thought life goes on. I have just been told my first-born son, only twenty years of age, has been killed and those people out there don't know.

'What time did it happen?'

'I don't know, but he was on his way to work,' said

Mr Newark. I was asleep till 10 a.m. that morning. Poor Mathew was in Heaven before I was awake.

Mr Newark arranged for a car to take me to Maureen's house, where she lives with my two other sons Michael, sixteen and Daniel, nineteen.

As we raced through the traffic the woman police officer who was driving spoke to me. A million thoughts race through your mind at a time like this. I told her that I had spent twenty-five years telling other people that they had lost someone, and I never thought it would happen to me. Why should I think I was so special?

Arriving at my sons' family home in Walton, I was met by Sergeant Moore, who had had the unfortunate task of telling Maureen and the boys. Everyone was distraught, as those of you who have been in this situation know. I tried to be strong and be as sensible as I could be in the circumstances; after all, I was the father, and yet my two sons Michael and Daniel were so brave. Thank you boys!

We had to go to the mortuary. Daniel has had a fear of hospitals all his life, he hates them. I asked him if he would come with us so we could say goodbye to Mathew as a family. I felt that was very important. Daniel agreed to come.

Arriving at the Coroner's offices at the hospital, we were shown into a small office. I asked to speak to the officer alone. I knew him as a work colleague from years ago when we were at Kingston together.

He explained to me how Mathew had been killed at about 8.30 that morning on his way to work at the very hospital where he now lay.

Mathew was minding his own business riding his 'pop-pop' moped (it couldn't even do thirty mph), as I called it. A car driving in the opposite direction, for some unknown reason, had gone out of control and collided with Mathew. His death was instantaneous.

As a family we entered the chapel and we saw Mathew. He looked as if he had a smile on his face. Daniel was uncontrollable and I went to usher him out. 'No, Dad. Can I be with him on my own for five minutes please.' Before we left Daniel on his own I said a prayer out loud. Daniel stayed on his own, and after a few minutes when he came out he seemed a different person.

When I later asked Daniel about this, he said that when he was told of Mathew's death he felt as if someone had ripped his insides out, but when he came out of that room, he felt as if someone had put them back in. Michael, too, had his own private time with Mathew, then we returned to their home.

It is really peculiar what goes on in your mind. I wanted to be the one to tell everyone. It was my responsibility; I am his father. I thought that when Mathew was taken to the hospital I should have been the one to undress him. I had done it when he was a baby – I should have done it then, so that he had no embarrassment.

I could write for hours, and pages and pages, and perhaps I will another time. I now know how important it is that I continue to work as a medium to be better than ever – to show that life continues to give evidence of the survival of the human spirit, as evidence has already been shown to me.

I realise how important it is to any person who has lost a loved one that the medium should be of good quality and that the best possible evidence should be obtained from the Communicator – as one day that Communicator may be my son Mathew and that recipient may be me.

Mathew had his own saying, which I know is borrowed, but is something he always maintained and practised: 'If you cannot say anything good, then say nothing.'

Mathew's only love in life was life itself and he spent most of his life helping others and thinking of others. Mathew was a 'giver'. We love you, Mathew.

There are things, practical things, you have to do when a loved one passes. Like, for instance, arrange the funeral. I'd never arranged a funeral before; how do you do it, where do you start, how much does it cost? At a time like this your mind is everywhere. So much to think of, so many people you want to care for.

I know I'm skipping millions of things I'd like to say. Particularly my thanks to so many people, including Mathew, who has already made himself known to us from Heaven. And the strength he has given to so many of us has helped us cope with his passing.

Mathew's service was held on Thursday, 24 November 1994. It was a beautiful occasion, conducted by Madge Summerfield and supported by Ray Robinson. So many people attended, estimated at between three to four hundred. The nice thing about it was that all of those people attended, not out of a sense of duty, but because they wanted to out of love and respect for him.

Mathew has not 'died', but just gone home to Heaven, where one day we will all be together again.

My son Michael received some inspired thoughts and I would just like to include some of these.

My Brother
We used to enjoy each other's company so sometimes we would go go-karting and really enjoy ourselves, or perhaps go fishing, or even at home we would sit down and watch a film, or TV as Mat would call it.

But above all I only realise now how much I loved, adored, appreciated and was so grateful for such a kind caring person's company and how lucky I was that he was, and still is, my brother.

*

Michael also wrote these words about Mathew's accident and entitled it, 'The Tragic Day – Or Was It?'

*

The day Mathew left this life was very sudden and obviously very sad, but in a funny sort of way we should be kind of happy because Mathew has just passed on to a very beautiful place where he has a job to do which I, and everybody else, knows is keeping all the children and older people all very happy.

Mathew has already sent me a message saying – sad to say but I had to choose some way to go – believe it or not it was a nice way to go, out in the open, riding my way to Heaven, if you like.

I was inspired to write these words while sitting and thinking of Mathew just three days after he passed.

God has not taken me from you for pain.
He has taken me for other People's gain
I fly the wind, I circle the sky
I am with you I did not die
I press the hungry that they should eat
I pressure the mighty that they might weep
I sow the seed in man's mind
To all creatures they shall be kind
I am with you in everything you see
A part of me lives inside you all
I am the life of the Smile on a thousand faces
The twinkle in children's eyes in a thousand places
The chuckle you hear in the corner of your mind
Is the place, I, you will always find
My time has come, my place fulfilled
Do not let your tears be spilled.

CHAPTER TWELVE

COLOUR READINGS

Imagine a world without colour! Impossible, isn't it, because colour is so much a part of our everyday experience. Colour brings the world to life on a canvas of reds, greens, yellows, greys, blues and browns and has such a profound effect, not only on the way we see our world, but on the way we relate to it emotionally – and to each other.

For as long as I can remember, I have known that colour is as important a part of my life as, for example, the sound of beautiful music. Both are emotional stimulants that keep me 'finely tuned' to this world of ours. When colour is dulled in my life, I am dulled too.

Don't we all experience this each year with the coming of Spring, bringing, as it does, an explosion of new life and colour into our lives? The effect on me, and probably most people, is sheer exhilaration once the dull grey skies of winter have been swept away.

There is no doubt that when God created this Earth, He proved himself to be a tremendous decorator! Look at the blue sky; yet it isn't blue – it can be grey, it can be black. The background in which we live is constantly changing, with many shades of colour.

Think how sick you would feel if you woke up one morning and found that everything was just one shade of pink.

Were you wearing the same coloured clothes a week ago as you are today?

Of course not. Apart from the fact some of the clothes you wore a week ago have by now probably found their way into your washing machine, the fact is that we dress each day according to our mood.

If we feel happy we probably want to wear something bright, as we also do if we want a pick-me-up. If we feel miserable, or worried, then a quieter colour will fulfil our emotional need better at that moment.

We do our best to feed on our need for colour in the way we dress ourselves, the way we present ourselves, even in the way we care for ourselves.

Next time you go shopping, be aware of the colours people choose for their cars; bright-coloured cars far outnumber dull, grey ones. This is another area of our lives where instinct and emotional needs are dictated by our subconscious.

Perhaps the most fundamental aspect of colour relates most intimately to each of us on this planet – through our aura. According to my dictionary, an aura is 'a supposed emanation of light surrounding a person, and visible to people claiming psychic powers'.

I see a person's aura in colours and I can only describe it as like an energy field that cocoons each of us in a gently swirling multi-coloured brightness.

The make-up of this aura is rather like a fingerprint, individual to each of us at any one time. The aura may change in substance, intensity of light and colours, according to our well-being and aspirations.

This being the case, I came to the conclusion that it should be possible to see the aura and use the predominant colours, along with my psychic perception to 'read' a person.

The more I studied colours and their meanings, the more fascinating it became, to the point where I began introducing colour readings in my psychic demonstrations around Britain. I stunned members of my audiences, as well as myself, with the sheer accuracy of what I was able to tell people about themselves, their past, their present and even their future. I was obtaining eighty-five to ninety per cent accuracy.

Colour became something of a game to me. I didn't even need to know, or see, the person for whom I was giving a colour reading. It was sufficient that the person wanting the reading just named the first three colours that came straight into his or her mind when asked. If the subject stopped and thought about it, then the 'test' was largely worthless.

However before I take you further into the fascinating world of colour, try to describe, for example, the colour 'red' to a man who has been blind from birth.

Don't tell him to imagine the warmth that comes from the sun, as in 'red hot', because he has not seen the sun. There is no reason why he should not regard 'hot' as blue or green or yellow.

What I am trying to say to you is that we take colours very much for granted. We have man-conceived meanings and relationships with them.

When you honestly think about it, it is impossible to explain 'green' to someone who has never set eyes on this or any other colour. In other words, we relate particular colours to particular things – green as grass, black as soot, brown as a berry.

What word comes to mind when I say 'pink'? Some people will say 'anger', some will say 'carnations', some might say 'a rocket'.

So, with colours, I can only give my own interpretation of what the 'trip words' might be to help you to use your psychic ability with colour readings. This is perhaps the easiest way to explore your own psychic perception, which I believe is within each one of us. This is how you play the game.

Look ahead to page 215 where I explain the meanings of a number of colours. These are not 'meanings', as such, but more 'trip words', which is the way I feel best describes them. Red indicates anger, yet it can also indicate stubbornness or *joie de vivre*, a love of life. This is where your own psychic perception comes into the interpretation of these colours.

When you are concentrating on a reading, certain trip words will spring out at you and so you deliver your reading using these particular words as stepping stones along your route.

Within a short time, you will find words coming from your mouth almost automatically and you may wonder how this is happening. It means that you are beginning to use your own psychic power.

To begin with, however, you will need some help, and this is where prompt cards will assist you.

Take six plain postcards and, on the front of each, write, in big, bold letters, six main colours – one colour on the front of each postcard. Now you will have six postcards with the name of a colour on each, for example RED ... YELLOW ... GREEN ... BLUE ... PINK ... ORANGE.

On the back of each card, write in note form the meanings or trip words that relate to each colour. These are to jog your memory until you become familiar with the meanings of each colour.

You are now ready to give a colour reading to one of your friends. Don't let it bother you that you may know him or her quite well. In all probability you will surprise yourself when, during the course of your reading, details about them flood into your head and from your mouth that even you were not aware of! It is quite uncanny.

Invite your friend to pick three cards and click your fingers, if necessary, to ensure that they do so spontaneously. Don't give them time to contemplate their response. Turn over each colour card in the order that it was picked, to reveal the trip words, and tell your friend that the card will help to guide you along the correct route in your reading.

For just a moment, study the red card and the words you have written on the back. Cast your eyes over them and be especially aware of any words that seem to jump out at you. Perhaps 'stubborn', 'loyalty' and 'heartburn' catch your eye. Concentrate on these words, and begin.

Your reading may go like this:

'There is a certain stubbornness about your attitude to both yourself and other people. It is as though you are afraid of being seen to be weak, to be the kind of person who easily gives in, so your stubbornness is really a form of self-defence. And yet you are also a very *loyal* person, so stubbornness is rather alien to your true character.

'Maybe, if you think about this, you will agree with me that it is possible that the stubborn part of your make-up conflicts with your loyal nature and can sometimes end up creating stress which shows itself as "heartburn".

'Yes, you do suffer occasionally from more than a normal dose of heartburn, so bring your stubborn nature under more control and perhaps you will also reduce your heartburn!'

In all probability your colour reading will have already engaged the full attention of your friend (we all like to hear about ourselves, don't we?) and I guarantee that by the time you have pursued the other two colours as well, at least fifteen minutes will have passed.

Don't be put off if the readings fail to flow quite as easily as I have suggested they will here. You may not be too satisfied but your subject may be much more curious and amazed by your readings than he or she will allow.

Just keep churning them out and see how quickly and easily the words begin to flow as you develop your psychic ability. It won't be long before you abandon your cards and work 'alone' as it were.

I like to use six colours. If there is an indication around the sixth colour that there is something about the person's future that they should know, then I ask for a seventh. Perhaps they are thinking of changing their job.

Let us say their next colour is black (not truly a colour, but with colour readings it is significant), then I tell them that this is not the right time to contemplate changing their job because black indicates the ending of a situation, not necessarily an ending as in death, but it might be a divorce or a failed romance.

This is still leaving the person rather in the air, so I request one more colour . . . ah, blue.

I can now tell them that the reason the change of job won't work out is that they are expecting help from another person and it will not materialise just at present as they are hoping. Black shows this.

As you get better, you can often tell from experience what colours people will give you next but do not be thrown by the know-it-all who tries to confuse you with 'off-pink' or 'dirty yellow', for example. Just accept the colour given and use it the way you feel is best for that person.

Lilac, violet-pink and cerise (a purplish-pink) are the kind of colours you will be given by those wanting to be awkward. Some people like to challenge. They want to see the look of despair on your face when they say 'cerise'. These people are not giving you a true reflection of themselves, so pass them by. Be equally, but politely, dismissive by telling them: 'I'll come back to you later.' And don't! People who genuinely want to help themselves will not muck about in this way.

Now for a breakdown of the six most popular colours. I have italicised the trip words you should write down on your cards.

Red

When someone choses red it normally shows that they are quite *strong* characters; that they like to *take charge*. They can be a bit *bossy*. There is a *stubbornness* about them. They are quite *single-minded*. They make good *leaders*. People who pick red have a *determination to succeed* in everything. They are *family-orientated*, in fact the backbone of their family unit, with great *strength of character*.

On the minus side, the person who selects red may suffer from an excessive *temper*, with a short fuse and a *low tolerance* level, especially when red is high up in their colour selection.

Another day this same person may feel less aggressive and red will not necessarily be their first choice. It may still be among the selection but in third or fourth place. This is quite normal because any colour selection, and therefore any colour reading, is largely applicable to only that moment in time. On an emotional level, it is the way that person feels there and then.

Red is the colour of *stress* and *blood pressure* problems (high, rather than low). If red is chosen as a priority choice, it could indicate that, as a child, this person may have suffered some *blood disorder*, or that their mother did.

Use your psychic ability to guide you over what, initially, may seem to be rather frightening colour-reading hurdles. Look at a person's clothes. If red is predominant, then you will know that they have a positive outlook on life, especially on that day. They are probably happy and want to be noticed.

Yellow
This is a crisp, clean colour, full of *optimism*. People who pick this one have high hopes for the way life is going for them. Yet they can be *daydreamers*. I would call them mental gypsies, inasmuch as their minds will always be *flitting* from one thought to another, one idea to another, always on the move, with no shortage of ideas!

If yellows use colour positively, they can become very *positive* about everything they do.

Yellow is a *doing colour*. It gets you moving because you *want to do things*. It is a great colour.

On the negative side, yellow tends to show up a

person's *nervous* disposition. Or it may be that the person who picks yellow is nervous about something which is happening in their life.

Green

This is a very *earthy* colour, as is brown which I will deal with later. Green is a colour that gives the feeling of *freedom*. Someone who chooses green will more than likely have a *family birthday* or anniversary *in March or November*. For instance, if a baby is expected in the family and your subject has chosen green, then it can reasonably be expected to arrive in March or November.

This is where you can test your psychic intuition a little more by choosing either March or November. Then you need to know a date in the month you have chosen. This is how to find it.

Break for a moment from your reading and allow your mind to go blank (shut your eyes if you wish) and imagine a blackboard in front of you.

'See' a number written on that blackboard. Let's say the number fourteen appears on your mental blackboard, then tell your friend the birthday is on, or around, the fourteenth.

The blackboard technique becomes more reliable the more you use it.

Not unnaturally, green is a colour which means *relaxation*. Those who choose it are very comfortable living, for example, in the *countryside*.

217

Or it could be that they were brought up on a farm in the countryside, alongside a green open space, perhaps a large park. Use your psychic intuition to be more specific.

Greens make *good friends*.

Royal Blue

A bold, positive blue, rather than wishy-washy pale blue. A good colour, it shows *reliability* in those who select it. There could be links with the *police*, the *armed forces* or someone who is a *disciplinarian*.

These people make *loyal* friends; people to whom others tend to tell their problems. They like to *assert* their *authority* and yet they will *listen* and *take note* of someone they respect. *Not as stubborn* as those who choose red.

Blue indicates quite a *soft nature*, a *very caring* person. *Nursing* would be an appropriate line of work for a true blue. Put *red and blue together* and you have a person with *strong family ties*, with the family being the most important aspect of their life.

Blue is a popular business-suit colour because it is *authoritative* and conveys the impression of someone who is in charge of themself and reliable. They like to have their affairs – and those of others – *sorted out*. They are quite good at making *money*, although not necessarily good at holding on to it! These are *confident* people.

Pink

This is a very *spiritual* colour; what I would call a 'little girl' colour. People who pick shades of pink tend to like *small things* in life. It could be a *relationship* which they enjoy, but they are certainly happier on a one-to-one basis rather than being 'lost' in a *crowd*. Excellent people to *sit and talk to*.

People who choose pink tend to have a lot of *patience*. It is also a colour of *learning* and might be the choice of someone at college or at school, or someone with fond memories of their learning years.

Think of pink in terms of *education and spirituality*; someone with a liking for *animals*. It also shows someone always *eager to expand their mind*, the kind of people, perhaps, who could learn to give excellent colour readings!

If your subject picks pink, he or she may be looking to the *future*, perhaps towards a *new job*. Pink indicates a *birth* and good times.

Mauve

Again, this shows spirituality. Depending on how high up the order the choice of mauve is, it could indicate a move towards life in the *church*. It may represent a move towards *marriage*.

There is, however, a certain *fierceness* about mauve and those who choose it, perhaps indicating a *strict upbringing*. Even so, mauve is a good colour, one which goes with *healing*.

For anyone sending out prayers, pink and mauve are creative colours, excellent for meditation. If you want to feel good at home, have mauve around you. It is a warm and secure colour.

Orange

A very *vibrant* colour. It is a fire sign and can indicate a *birthday* or *anniversary* *in August*. Those who choose orange tend to be involved in the arts. They may be *performers* themselves, quite *strong* and always prepared to *experiment*. In fact, they would probably be competent artists.

In choice of occupation, they would probably gravitate towards *design work*, *fashion*, *architecture* (even *cooking*) where they can express their *creativity*, especially when yellow is also selected.

These people must be given their head in a job situation or they will quickly lose interest.

Brown

This is another *earthy* colour. Someone who picks this one will probably have reached a rather *stagnant*, perhaps *boring*, time in their life. They will feel too *rooted*. Brown is an indication that this is about to *change*. Perhaps it is a change in their *home*, in their *job*, in *family circumstances*. Maybe a change in the person *themself* and the way they look at things. People who choose brown are *solid* and *reliable*.

Again, I must stress that you will need to *read* the

thoughts that come into your mind as you concentrate on your subject's choice of brown, and the interpretations of the trip words given here.

Light Blue

If someone says 'light blue', it tends to show they would be *good in a group* and that they do not particularly like to take charge. They like to be *led* a little. Normally *nice-natured*, very *kind* people, though a little *powdery*.

All the right ingredients are there, it's just that these ingredients need whipping up into something a little more interesting! They need just a bit more strength of character. Light blue people tend to suffer excessively from *colds*.

Black

This is the choice of the *deep thinker*. If black is chosen, they may be facing the *end of a situation*.

Some people think of black as meaning death but I like to think of it more as 'closing a chapter' of their lives, *turning the corner* of a sequence of events. Certainly *not doom and gloom*.

In fact, it can mean the end of a lethargic stage of their life and moving on to a new, more interesting stage.

It could also mean that this person has recently 'lost' somebody, again not necessarily in death but through a *divorce*, the *end of a romance* or the end of a job. Think of black in terms of a full stop or a comma, where things can *change direction*. Contemplate a *December anniversary*.

White
This shows a *negative* period in one's life. Not a tremendously popular choice. It means *cleanliness*.

Silver
These people like to feel *secure*. It can also mean that there is an *anniversary*, perhaps a *wedding*, coming up shortly.

You will develop your own 'feel' about other colours and shades of colours. Note them down on your cards as you build up your knowledge of their meanings to you.

I have suggested that, initially, you should ask your subjects for only three colours, but, as you are able to interpret more colours, so you can invite a wider choice – perhaps up to six.

However, to begin with, stick to the three. To ring the changes, you can divide the person's age by three and tell them that their first card will deal with the first ten years of their life, the second from ten to twenty and the third from twenty to thirty.

If they want to know about their future, then ask them to choose a fourth card.

Remember, whatever you choose to do, you are

using your psychic intuition to bring the chosen colours to life and to make them meaningful.

Once you start to feel what various colours say for you, in relation to that person, you are beginning to use this game on a psychic level.

CHAPTER THIRTEEN

PSYCHIC STATES OF AMERICA!

I know it's a challenge but I believe I am up to it. I want to return to America to help the people of that great country to understand and believe in a life after death that is as real in spirit as this one on Earth is to the living.

Unfortunately, although Americans are very much into religion, most of them don't take an interest in the work of mediums like myself because they haven't had the opportunity to take a genuine interest in spiritualism. Those who do go right over the top!

I want to change all that. I can give them a clear insight into the real life beyond this one which they will all, without exception, be a part of one of these days.

In America the jokers will snigger that the work of mediums is only appreciated by the retired people of Florida and California, because they are closest to the hereafter! If this is the case, then the elderly residents of Miami and Los Angeles must be the most enlightened in America, as well as the most psychic-targeted members of the great American population. Because of their beliefs they are the most vulnerable to those looking for easy, and rich, pickings.

I was in the States in 1988 on a relatively short visit, but the thing that struck me most was the large number of screwball gospellers and so-called psychics pouring out their platitudes about Heaven when all they were really interested in was lining their pockets with dollars. Religion in the USA is a business, a multi-billion-dollar business. There's very little sincerity.

Having said that, what I do admire about Americans is their openness, even their brashness. They are not afraid to air their views, whatever their beliefs. They have an honesty that is almost child-like in its innocence.

This is why I feel they would be ready to hear what

I have to say, however controversial I might appear to be. At least I would be sincere.

In Britain, if anyone goes against the grain, they get their knuckles wrapped – no doubt as I will get mine wrapped for speaking out against the dullness of British spiritualism and some of the leading lights in it.

In Britain we have had many visits from American Christian and psychic gospellers and campaigners, telling us how to run our lives. Now I want to take my own, very British brand of spiritual survival philosophy to the Americans to offer them an alternative. I want to do it on a grand scale, to get noticed, make a lot of noise and be heard from Miami to Washington DC.

Let them try to shoot me down. I don't care. What I want is worth fighting for and I want the ears of the American people.

The Yanks like entertainers, so I'll lay on psychic entertainment for them in Miami or New York, wherever they will have me. I know that my psychic evenings attract big audiences. I will need to be seen on television, heard over the radio, written up in the newspapers. The power and influence of the American media are mind-blowing.

In the same way that people have their own coloured auras, so I believe that regions can reflect different auras; countries, too.

One of my ambitions is to persuade an American

broadcasting company to give me airtime so that I can put out daily, countrywide psychic forecasts, rather on the lines of weather forecasts, breaking the predictions down into regions.

'California, you are under the influence of yellow today. You ladies be sure to wear something yellow when you go out shopping to give you that complete feeling today!

'Fellas, get your secretary to fill your office with yellow flowers and you'll glow through the day, pulling off some of your best deals.'

Get the idea? Florida might be under the influence of blue, in which case I'd have to tell the business-men there to expect more meetings than usual and to be especially flexible in their ideas and those they discuss.

I wouldn't suggest that anyone put their business or their personal life on the line with such psychic forecasts. They'd be what I might call serious fun!

I think the Americans would go for it because they know how to handle fun and they accept innovation. They don't necessarily have to understand it to appreciate it. They just give it a chance.

To a large degree, spiritualism in Britain is standing still and I need to move forward to spread my psychic philosophy beyond these shores. Spirit tells me that America is the country where I should be.

Look what they have right now – a lot of crackpot psychics talking a lot of rubbish. Then there are other great entertainers like Shirley MacLaine talking about aliens in her books and on the air. Uri Geller is psychic but he seems more interested in finding oil wells and is probably better known for bending spoons than for asking the American people to think about life after death.

It seems to me that mediums are losing out on the one thing that is missing in America – genuine clairvoyance put across as serious entertainment.

I would start with three months in Miami where psychics almost rule people's lives. Having conquered Miami, and become noticed, I would want to take my show to all the big cities: Boston, New York, Los Angeles, San Francisco. Everyone would have a great time! I'd get across my message of spiritual hope and life everlasting but I'd use entertainment as the vehicle to do it.

In America, the time for a new spiritual revival is now. It just needs the right person to take the right kind of psychic message to this huge country to trigger off a psychic revolution. I know I am the person to do it!

I will do it through the cream of American show-business. I will sit down with Shirley MacLaine, Rod Stewart, Clint Eastwood, Mel Gibson, Elizabeth Taylor, Michael Jackson and so many more. I know, for example, that Jackson's biggest problem is his loneliness and I can help him. Michael should be wearing more blue and more purple, strong in mind healing. He should wear much less black and white, negative colours which are not for him.

I would like to sit down with Priscilla Presley because I think she would soon realise that I know her probably even better than she knows herself! She had a love/hate relationship with Elvis, perhaps one that was even a little bit cruel to her, although I am sure she would find it hard to describe it this way. Maybe I could reveal other secrets to Priscilla Presley which would impress her but that is for her to be told privately, not for me to publish.

The task I have set myself in America will not be easy. There could be considerable opposition from the likes of glitzy Beverly Hills psychic Kebrina Kincade who might see me as a British upstart trespassing on her patch. If she is so good, however, then she will have nothing to fear from me.

Kebrina is the blonde bombshell who warned two friends, Anwar Sadat (President of Egypt) and Princess Fatya, that they were about to die. Two weeks later they were dead. Sadat was assassinated and Fatya was shot by her husband.

Kebrina went on television proud about her psychic prowess over both predictions, and said, rather glibly, that if people will not listen to her warnings they have only themselves to blame when the worst happens. Some consolation if you're dead! I don't approve of giving death warnings. I regard it as bad mediumship.

But then Kincade is part of the Los Angeles psychic

set which has roped in just about every section of the superstitiously vulnerable Hollywood showbusiness community. It seems many of them will believe absolutely anything. For example, if I stood on stage in front of a British audience and began wailing and whistling like a demented dolphin, then said I was the soul of this dolphin talking to them through Keith Charles, they'd fall off their seats laughing! And who would blame them!

Does that sound too far-fetched? Sadly, it isn't because they have a guy in Los Angeles who holds his audience spellbound as the soul of this super-friendly dolphin speaks to them and gives them messages through the human communicator. Plain daft, I call it. I'd like to set American psychic investigator James Randi on this one. He would have a field day.

Then there is a young woman who calls herself 'Mafu'.

I have seen Penny Torres Rubin slip into the most untrance-like trance imaginable, flex her body and pose like a man (presumably this Mafu) and, in a silly voice (again, presumably Mafu's), hold an audience of fifty men and women spellbound with her profound messages.

Our Penny makes a pretty penny herself (or should I say, buck) with her Oscar-winning performances. At one such demonstration of Mafu's psychic power, I saw her caressing the face of a dark-haired young man who was totally under her spell, and brushing back the hair of the young woman standing alongside him. She whispered, huskily: 'You are one sexy guy!' then went on to tell him he should make great love with the woman by his side. The young man didn't bat an eyelid; the young woman burst into tears, overcome with emotion!

I was nearly sick over the whole pathetic saga. This was supposed to be a spirit guide full of wisdom. It left me speechless and not a little angry.

However, when you have celebrities such as Zsa Zsa Gabor telling people how 'desperately psychic' she is herself, I suppose you cannot really blame the Mafus of Hollywood for jumping on the bandwaggon.

Jacqueline Stallone, Sylvester's mum, calls herself a psychic astrologer and, wearing a sausage-size gold headband, looks every bit the part in her fashionable Beverly Hills home. She wanted to find her boy so that he could verify just how good she was in her predictions. She spent a couple of hours on the telephone trying to find out where he'd got to.

However, Hollywood is where it's all happening and where I believe there is a place for me. This British-based 'psychic cop', with a mission to clean up the psychic hot spots in cities like Los Angeles, is ready to demonstrate just what mediumship is really all about. I feel sure the Los Angeles police would be in favour.

CHAPTER FOURTEEN

SHOWBUSINESS 'SHORTS'

Leslie Caron, actress
'When you die, that's it. You're just a lump of meat!'
. . .

Sherrie Hewson, actress
'Ghosts seem to have followed me around much of
my life. But I have never tried to make contact. I
don't think there is anything I could do to help.'
. . .

Dean Martin, actor
The 1987 death of his thirty-five-year-old son, Dean Paul, in an air crash devastated Dean Martin. 'I am just looking forward to seing my son in Heaven,' he said at the time. When his close friend Sammy Davis Jnr died three years later, Dean commented: 'Look how horrible and public Sammy's death was, we are all just waiting to die.'

. . .

Bob Hoskins, actor
His acting career could have been triggered off by his meeting with the spirit of a Benedictine nun when he was working as a porter in London's Covent Garden.

'I was in the cellar when, on the wall, appeared a woman's face. She was wearing a nun's habit and reaching out to me with outstretched hands. She spoke but I couldn't hear what she said. Later, I learned that Covent Garden was once called Convent Garden and was owned by the Benedictines of Westminster. The story was that whoever saw the nun's face would have a very lucky life from that day on,' said Mr Hoskins.

. . .

Dave Prowse, actor
An actor, and Britain's strongest man in the sixties, Dave made his mark in the film world as evil Darth

Vader in the film *Star Wars*. He owns and runs his own health club in south London, which is haunted by the ghost of a tramp murdered in the building a hundred years ago. 'We call him Bluff. He does barbell workouts overnight when the gymnasium is locked up,' says Dave. 'A couple of times members who kipped down in the room above the padlocked gym have been rudely woken up by terrible bangings and crashings from below. On investigation they found equipment scattered around the gymnasium! One of these members fled for his life and never returned!'

. . .

Nick Berry, actor
Asked if he believes in Heaven, he said: 'No, Heaven is a wonderful idea, but I'm afraid I don't believe it exists.'

. . .

Lynsey de Paul, television celebrity
She says she lived with a ghost for seven years and had this advice about being companionable with a spook. 'Treat your ghost gently!' According to Lynsey, unless it is a true blue poltergeist, and she says there are very few of these, a ghost won't hurt you!

. . .

235

Todd Carty (Mark Fowler in BBC-TV's EastEnders*)*
Asked for his views on the afterlife, he said: 'We all get spiritual feelings now and again, or *déjà vu*, and I'd like to know where they come from. I'd love to believe that when I pop my clogs there'll be something coming after. I have an open mind.'

. . .

Mike Myers (who starred in Wayne's World*)*
When his Liverpool-born dad, Eric, died, Mike honoured his father's last wish to have his ashes scattered on the River Mersey. New York-based Mike told friends that he had spoken to his dad in the spirit world. Describing himself as 'a low-grade psychic', Mike said: 'I wanted to meet my dad again so I went into a meditative state and am convinced I talked to him. Dad asked me who I wanted to talk to from the spirit world and he brought Peter Sellers. I had a good chat with him, too.'

. . .

Diana West, actress
Asked if she believed in life after death, she said, 'Yes, I think we go somewhere else, but I don't think we come back. I believe that you can contact people who've died – I met a violent poltergeist when I was a child. Dead friends have come to me and said goodbye when I've been half-asleep.'

. . .

Tracy Dawson, widow of comedian Les Dawson
A year after his death, Tracy said Les's ghost still happily haunted their family home in Lytham, Lancashire, where Les lived for twenty years before his death in 1993.

Tracy said Les's ghost sings as he moves around the house, hits keys on the piano and moves ornaments and pictures. 'I am not psychic, but I feel happy he is around and finding ways of reminding me he is still here,' said Tracy.

. . .

Joanna Lumley, actress
She told the *Daily Mail*: 'I don't think you can help being reincarnated, whether you believe in it or not. You're going to be recycled, let's put it like that, in some way. Whether I will come back as me, Joanna Lumley, into the spirit of a something or other I'm not sure, but I certainly can remember things that have never happened to me, places I've been to, this *déjà vu* thing or the sudden closeness you feel to people you don't know.'

. . .

Anna Nicole Smith, actress and Marilyn Monroe lookalike
She believes the ghost of Marilyn Monroe watches over her.

237